If Love Were Oil, I'd Be About a Quart Low

"IF YOU LOVE GRIZZARD, YOU WILL WEEP FOR HIM IN THIS BOOK. BUT YOU'LL ALSO LAUGH YOUR OVERALLS OFF."
—*Anderson Independent-Mail*, **South Carolina**

"A wonderfully warm look at growing up, love, marriage (three), divorce (three again) and the Oedipus complex . . . highly recommended."
—*Tulsa Tribune*, **Oklahoma**

"Serious and tender without sinking into sentimentality . . . Grizzard's greatest gift is his ability to shift gears quickly, to go from knee-slapping humor to something deadly serious in the blink of an eye."
—*Chattanooga Times*, **Tennessee**

"You'll find yourself chuckling a lot, laughing out loud, and ultimately clutching your sides, enjoying every minute of it."
—*Lamont Reporter*, **California**

"A page turner . . . will raise your own oil level up to the full mark."
—*Americus Times-Recorder*, **Georgia**

"Shows tenderness and poignancy . . . his talent transcends the creating of sometimes humorous, sometimes biting, always entertaining columns."
—*Pensacola Journal*, **Florida**

ALSO BY LEWIS GRIZZARD

Kathy Sue Loudermilk, I Love You

Won't You Come Home, Billy Bob Bailey?

Don't Sit Under the Grits Tree
With Anyone Else But Me

They Tore Out My Heart and Stomped
that Sucker Flat

Elvis is Dead and I Don't Feel So Good Myself

Published by
WARNER BOOKS

If Love Were Oil, I'd Be About a Quart Low

LEWIS GRIZZARD
ON WOMEN

WARNER BOOKS

A Time Warner Company

This Warner Books Edition is published by arrangement with Peachtree Publishers, Ltd., 494 Armour Circle, N.E., Atlanta, Georgia 30324

Cover photo by Charlie Archambault

Warner Books, Inc.
1271 Avenue of the Americas
New York, N.Y. 10020

 A Time Warner Company

Printed in the United States of America

First Warner Books Printing: December, 1986

15 14 13 12 11

DEDICATION

This book is dedicated to the memory of Capt. Lewis McDonald Grizzard, Sr., who fought the Germans, the North Koreans, and the Communist Chinese, and later said to me, "Son, there's nothing in this world meaner than a quarrelsome woman."

I

Deception Wears Nylon Hose

M Y FATHER ALWAYS had a great deal of trouble with women, too. When he was a young man, growing up in Gwinnett County, Georgia, he opened a hot dog stand on the side of a country road. A few days later, two women in an Essex coupe came over the hill, lost control of their car, and ran over my father's fledgling place of business.

"There wasn't an onion left," is how he later described the damage to me.

After that, he got a job calling bingo numbers at the local Moose Club. He was fired, however, when it was discovered that he was rigging games as a trade-out for favors from a young female bingo participant.

My father might have made it in the night club business, his next venture, had it not been for Lucille Wellmaker. He opened a little spot that featured beer for ten cents a glass and a jiving jukebox that offered six plays for a quarter. The combination, however, violated a basic rule of business: Never mix cheap beer and music. Lucille came in late one night and wanted to dance. She was a big, country girl who wore what my father described as "Bermuda-alls" —overalls cut off at the knee.

The trouble began when Lucille asked a fellow named Spud Kemp to dance, and Spud refused on the basis that Lucille was uglier than a "bastard billy goat," if I recall my father's exact terminology in recounting the event.

"Lucille," he said, "reached down in one of the legs of her Bermuda-alls and pulled out a sawed-off wagon spoke and turned the place out. She whipped everything and everybody in there, and then took on three deputy sheriffs when they came to arrest her. What was left of my jukebox," my father said, "you could have put in a paper sack."

My father was easily deceived by women, too. Once he went to see his older brother, my Uncle Frank, try a case. Uncle Frank was a marvelous criminal attorney with a booming voice that was a compelling mixture of Churchill's British, Tex Ritter's growling twang, and enough Barry Fitzgerald Irish on the tip end of the tongue to suggest there was some playful devilment to the man.

Frank was defending a fellow accused of making moonshine.

"Ladies and gentlemen of the jury," he began his summation, "the defense will stip-u-let (Fitzgerald) my client made a little eel-lee-gull (Ritter) whiskey, but just enough to keep body and soul to-gethah (Churchill)..."

Each time Uncle Frank raised his voice for emphasis, a

young woman sitting on the front row of the courtroom would howl in anguish. Uncle Frank convinced the jury to find his client innocent, and my father was deeply impressed.

"Frank," he said, "that was a beautiful job you did. But wasn't it pitiful about the man's wife?"

"Wife? What wife?" asked Uncle Frank.

"The man's wife who sat down front and cried," explained my father.

"That wasn't his wife," said Frank. "That was some ol' gull I paid fifty dolluhs to come heah and squall."

Like I said, he was easily deceived. As a matter of fact, I am who I am because my father fell into the deceptive trap of a woman—or of two women, to be exact. This story deserves some backgrounding.

My father's mother was Mary Eugenia McDonald Grizzard. She died eleven months before I was born. They tell me, however, she was a tiny, soft little woman, delicate to hold. She married a raucous old galoot by the name of Augustus Adolphus Grizzard in Gwinnett County, and she bore him twelve children, five of whom were male. They were Frank, Walter, John Wesley, Joe Brown, and my father, Lewis. Frank was a lawyer, of course. Walter and John Wesley were used car dealers of some renown. Joe Brown died young. My father was the baby of the family.

They tell me my grandmother had a special feeling for her baby boy. She didn't cut his curly locks until he was twelve, and he was further special to her because he could sing, and play piano, and tell funny stories with such ability that he was in great demand around the county for weddings, and funerals, and to drop by to pep up the sick and the dying.

Lewis eventually found a career as a soldier, and they tell me it was Miss Genie's one desire in the last years of her life that she live long enough to see her baby boy come home from World War II. She died soon after she was granted that wish.

My maternal grandmother, Willie Smith, was a fine sprout of a girl when she was sixteen and growing up in her father John Smith's fields in Heard County, Georgia, which is located on the western border of the state and notable for the fact that it was, and remains today, the only one of Georgia's one hundred and fifty-nine counties without a single mile of railroad tracks running through it.

Heard County was also known for its poor farmers and foot-washing Baptists. Willie Smith's family fell into both categories. Willie's cheekbones rode classically high on her face, her form was full, and there was a promise in her eyes that drew restless farm boys from miles around to seek her favor as she reached her sixteenth year. Her father, Old Man John Smith, often deemed it necessary to take his buggy whip to the most persistent of her callers.

However, when rawboned, hard-working, foot-washing, God-fearing Charles Bunyon Word began to call, Old Man John took a liking to the boy, and so did Willie, and she married him and gave him five children.

Johnny was first. He would become a doctor. Next came Jessie, a daughter; she married a man who had a job at the mill. Then came Christine, who wanted to be a teacher. She was followed by Hugh Dorsey, who was much more comfortable behind a plow than a book; he farmed. Una

Mae was the baby; she couldn't wait to get herself out of Heard County.

Christine, the third of the children, was a tall, gangly child with dark hair and deep, green eyes. She went off to Berry College in Rome, Georgia, to be educated, and afterwards she moved to the then-sleepy state capital of Atlanta. Teaching jobs in Georgia have always paid a paltry wage, and Christine soon discovered that she could keep a better roof over her head as a clerk.

Little sister Una Mae split from the family home down in the country and joined Christine in Atlanta. Both the Word girls, Christine and Una—she dropped the "Mae" the minute she crossed the county line—were dazzling beauties, and their callers came in droves.

One was none other than Lewis Grizzard, Sr., a rather handsome young man himself. It was Una Word who had first caught his eye. He asked her out for an evening and she agreed to go. He would call at the house where she and Christine shared a small apartment.

These, remember, were not women desperate for male companionship, however. A vast number of suitors were vying for their charms. Before my father-to-be arrived to fetch Una, she received and accepted what she felt was a better offer.

The plan was a simple one. Women have been using it for years. It went like this:

Lewis rang the doorbell. Christine answered it.

"Una's not here," she said.

"Not here?" asked the surprised caller.

"Her grandmother died and she had to rush home to the funeral."

"Who are you?"

"Her sister."

"You're not going to the funeral?"

"What funeral?"

"Your grandmother's."

Christine was impressed by the young man's ability to assume correctly that if one sister had been called home to her grandmother's funeral, something was strange about the fact that the other sister had chosen to remain behind.

Christine looked him over, liked what she saw, and decided to take advantage of her sister's obvious mistake in turning him down for another opportunity.

"If you want to know the truth," said Christine, "Una really had to get her false teeth fitted. She doesn't want anybody to know she has to wear false teeth."

"Una has false teeth?" he asked.

"Bad gums," said Christine, setting the hook further.

"What about your teeth?" the young man asked.

"All mine," said Christine. "Come on in."

They married a year later.

Soon afterwards came the beginning of World War II, and Lewis joined the infantry. He was three years away from his bride, Christine. His war record was impressive, to say the least. He received a battlefield commission, a Purple Heart, and a Bronze Star.

Lt. Lewis McDonald Grizzard, Sr., came marching home from war in 1945. He was stationed at Ft. Benning, Georgia, near Columbus, one hundred miles from Atlanta, where Christine (who had inherited her parents' frugality) had remained in order to keep her job. With returning soldiers ballooning the nation's work force, jobs were hard to come by.

Lewis, meanwhile, took a bed in the bachelor officer's quarters at Ft. Benning. Each Friday he would board the Central of Georgia's crack passenger train, the Man o' War, in Columbus, and spend the weekend with Christine in Atlanta.

There was a large problem here, however. Una had also married a returning soldier, and she and her husband were sharing the small apartment with Christine. So crowded were the premises that when Lewis came to visit, there were no opportunities whatsoever for either couple to engage in any sort of marital bliss.

Young Lewis, just back from three years at war, was slowly going out of his mind, and once again found himself a puppet on a female string. However, this was one time he refused to be dangled any longer. After several weeks of this agony, he stepped off the train at Atlanta's Terminal Station one evening, caught the streetcar to the apartment, and called his wife outside.

"Hear me out," he said. "Either you go back to Ft. Benning with me, or I want a divorce."

Good for him! There comes a time when a man must either assert himself or allow a woman to drive him straight up the dreaded tree of celibacy. Christine said goodbye to Una and her husband, packed her bags, and caught the next train to Columbus and Ft. Benning.

*   *   *

I always have had a thing for trains. I realize now that I got it honestly. After I became a grown man, it occurred to me that I would like to know the complete details of my birth. I'm not talking about finding out what color rubber gloves the doctor wore when he delivered me; I'm talking about I wanted to know under just what circumstances I was conceived. It should be the right of every American to know such, unless he or she feels that being told this information might indicate they were not exactly the result of planned parenthood, as in, "Well, one night your father came home drunk, and . . ."

I was willing to take this risk, however, and so one day when I was old enough not to be embarrassed in front of my mother that I knew about such things, I asked her how she came to be pregnant. The former Christine Word spared me all the details, but she did indicate that my father was in such a state of anxiousness on that train ride back to Columbus, that there is an excellent chance that somewhere out on the Central of Georgia high iron, as the crack Man o' War cut its way southward out of Atlanta, my parents broke the ground that spawned me. At any rate, whenever someone asks me what sign I was born under, I usually tell them that if one considers the moment of conception as the actual date of first life, I may have been introduced into this world under the sign that reads, "Dining Car in Opposite Direction."

*   *   *

As I look back on my roots, three things come to mind:

1. Some of my troubles involving females later in my life may have stemmed from some deep, psychological wounds that were inflicted upon me during my nine months in my mother's womb. Who says that a developing em-

bryo, once it gets ears, can't hear what's going on in the outside world?

After my mother got pregnant, my father indicated to her that if he had his say, he would take a baby girl. Perhaps I picked up on my father's preference even before I was born, and came into this world with a sense of resentment for women because of a feeling I had failed my father by not being one.

Why my own father would want a baby girl over a baby boy is not clear to me, but perhaps it was because he wanted to spare me the lifelong frustrations one must endure when dealing with women as a member of the opposite sex. My father even had a name for me, had I been a girl. They were going to call me Dawn. It could have been worse, of course. It could have been Lucille.

I was born on October 20, 1946, at the Army hospital in Ft. Benning, Georgia, county of Chattahoochee. My parents hadn't counted on the fact that I might be male, so they didn't have any good names picked out for a boy. In desperation, they simply gave me my father's name and stuck a "Jr." on the end of it.

I was one ounce shy of six pounds when I was born. I also apparently was an unattractive infant. When my Aunt Una saw me, she said to my Aunt Jessie, "Don't tell her I said this, but I think there is something terribly wrong with Christine's baby."

There would be many other women to make the same remark, even after Christine's baby grew into adulthood.

* * *

2. The problems most men have with women usually stem from their mothers. Their mothers love them and wait on them and wipe away their tears and forgive their every fault, and basically spoil them rotten. Men then go out into the world unprepared to deal with other women. They expect other women with whom they have an intimate relationship to be like their mothers—to hand squeeze their orange juice and cook French fries exactly as they like them, and to stick closely beside them, even when they do something totally inconsiderate and irrational. This, of course, is rarely the case. Frustrations and misunderstandings and violence, as was the case with Lucille Wellmaker and my father's jukebox joint, often result.

3. Women, without a doubt, have had a far greater influence on my life than have men. Women have provided the most joy in my life. Women have caused me the most pain. They have scratched my back when it itched. They have rubbed my head when it hurt. They have dazzled my eyes, befuddled my brain, and broken my heart.

It is true, in retrospect, that Adam would have been better off had he never laid eyes on Eve. But without her, Eden's gardens would have been nothing more than a lonely place in which to spend eternity, and the world never would have had nylon.

II

Constipation and
the Dreaded
Copperheaded
Water Rattler

ONE OF MY very first memories involves a tricycle accident that I had when I was perhaps three years old. I pedaled my tricycle off the front porch of our house. I don't recall why I did something so foolish, but I do recall learning from the experience that if I cried as long and as loud as I possibly could, my mother soon would arrive on the scene and ease whatever trauma had befallen me.

She picked me up, held my aching head, and then gave me ice cream so that I would stop crying. Whenever I wanted ice cream after that, I would pedal my tricycle off our front porch. My mother eventually caught on to that trick; had she not, I might have wound up with severe brain damage, all in the name of two large scoops of chocolate ice cream.

Women do have a way of caring for a man when he is injured or ill. When I had a stomachache, my mother brought me ginger ale. Ginger ale will do wonders for an aching stomach, especially if it has been poured over ice your mother has placed inside a towel and beaten with a hammer in order to crush it. When I had a cold, she brought me chicken noodle soup and promised that if I ate it all, I could have Fig Newtons for dessert. It's amazing how much chicken noodle soup a small boy can stand, if there is the promise of Fig Newtons afterwards.

No matter how old a man gets, the surest cure for his ills is to have a woman around to treat him like a little boy, because as soon as a man feels the slightest thing wrong with his health, he immediately reverts to his earliest childhood.

"I feel terrible," he whines.

"Where does my little precious hurt?"

"It's my head."

"It's his precious little head."

"It hurts bad."

"I know it does. Let Mommy kiss it and make it all better."

And it always does feel better when a woman kisses it.

The only time a man should *not* tell a woman he isn't feeling well is when he has the slightest hint that he might be constipated.

When I was a child, my mother constantly interrogated me regarding the state of my bowels. Regardless of what my symptoms might be, she first suspicioned they were the direct result of constipation. If my stomach hurt, she was certain I was constipated. If my head ached, constipation was the cause of it. If I became irritable, what I needed was a good bowel movement.

My mother spent hundreds, perhaps even thousands, of dollars on laxatives during my formative years. At first, she tried to trick me into taking them by offering me chocolate-flavored laxatives. I soon caught on to that ploy, however. I still don't eat anything that is chocolate-flavored if I am going to have to leave my house at any point in the ensuing eighteen hours.

What else my mother did, when she thought I was constipated, was tell the entire world about it. I was with her on a grocery shopping trip once.

"You certainly are a cute little boy," the man weighing vegetables said to me.

"He'll look better when he gets some of his color back," my mother, picking at the tomatoes, replied. "He's been constipated, you know."

"I didn't know," said the man weighing vegetables.

"Oh, yes," my mother continued. "First he started to get irritable, and then. . . ."

I tried to hide my head under the butter bean and eggplant bins. Not only had my mother embarrassed me beyond belief by telling the man I had been constipated, she further insisted on giving him every detail involving my stoppage.

The same thing happened to me when I started school. I was out a couple of days and my mother sent the first grade teacher a note that read, "Please excuse Lewis. He's been terribly constipated, and so I went and bought a box of supposi. . . ."

Every little boy in America can grow up to be president,

they taught me in school. But I didn't want to be president. They would interview my mother and she would tell the entire Washington press corps that the reason I had asked Congress for a tax hike probably was because I was constipated at the time.

I suppose, however, it is the sworn duty of nearly every mother to look after her children, even their bowel habits. In fact, were it not for my mother's hovering attention, I might have died a small boy, from a snakebite, of all things.

We remained in Ft. Benning a couple of years after I was born, and then my father received orders to report to Camp Chaffee, Arkansas. That's where the great tricycle crashes took place. That is also where I came into contact with my first—and almost last—snake.

We had a small garage near our house. My mother kept her wringer washing machine there. One morning, while she folded her clothes, I played in the dirt that was the garage floor.

My mother heard a strange, buzzing sound, looked up, and in her horror saw a large rattlesnake only a few feet away from me. It was coiled to strike. Not being aware of the dangers of snakes at my tender age, I showed no apparent intention of trying to remove myself from my perilous position.

As a matter of fact, all I did was sit there like an idiot, eating dirt. My mother screamed out and, in one quick motion, moved toward me and picked me up and whisked me away from the garage and the snake. A road gang was working nearby. One of the guards came and shot the snake.

As much as I was indebted to my mother for saving my life for the first time—there would be other opportunities for her to do the same thing—the snake incident had profound effects on my childhood. One, my mother didn't allow me out of the house alone for several years afterwards. Two, when she did allow me out of her sight, she usually did so with a long warning about looking for snakes. And three, all that combined to make me deathly afraid of any member of the reptile family, especially snakes, but also including lizards and turtles.

When I was older, I went on my first camping trip.

"Make certain," said my mother, "that you check your tent and sleeping bag for snakes."

I did just that. Every hour on the hour, I turned my sleeping bag inside out to make certain no snakes had crawled inside, and then I beat the sides of my tent with a large stick to frighten away any other snakes.

"What are you doing?" asked the adult who was supervising the camping trip.

"Running all the snakes out of my tent," I said.

"There aren't any snakes in your tent," he insisted.

"I know," I said. "I just ran them all out."

I have kept this fear of snakes all my life. I stay out of tall weeds, murky water, and the reptile house at the zoo. I don't believe there are snakes that won't bite you, and I don't believe the old axiom that snakes won't bite underwater. Of course, snakes will bite underwater, especially the dreaded copperheaded water rattler, which is so mean that if you check into a Holiday Inn, it will check into the room next to you and then bite you when you go in the pool.

Despite the fact there is a chance you will become paranoid about such things as snakes, having a mother to look after you offers a certain amount of comfort that a man misses when he leaves his mother's nest. I can't imagine growing up without a mother to nurse my ills and save me from tricycle accidents and snakes. Yet I was almost confronted with that very situation.

My mother contracted some sort of rare condition while we lived in Arkansas. It began with an itching scalp. Then her scalp became infected, and they put her in an Army airplane and flew her to Walter Reed Hospital in Washington, D.C. My father and I followed by train.

My mother lost all of her hair. The infection got worse. The doctors thought she was going to die. I can recall visiting her in the hospital. She had bandages all over her head. My father tried to explain the situation. I didn't understand him.

"Your mother is going to go away, son," he said.

"To where, Daddy?" I asked.

"To heaven," he said.

"Why can't we go?"

"We can later."

Heaven. Where was this heaven? What was this heaven? Why couldn't I go there with her? Who was going to hold me when I needed holding? Who was going to give me ice cream when I cried?

My mother didn't die. She didn't have any hair for a long time, but she didn't die. And when her hair grew back months later, it was very special to me, and I would sit in her lap for hours, or lie beside her while she slept, and twirl it back and forth between my fingers.

My mother was even more dedicated to my well-being after her close bout with death. She had had a dream, or at least she thought it was a dream, during her most desperate hours in the hospital. She would tell me the story later:

"In the dream," she began, "I was standing by a beautiful lake, and you were playing in the flowers and shrubs around it. I heard a voice from the other side of the lake. I looked and I saw someone talking to me. The voice was telling me, 'Go back. Don't cross the lake. Your little boy needs you.'"

The voice, she said, was Miss Genie's, my father's mother, my paternal grandmother, who had died eleven months before I was born. They called it a miracle that my mother had lived.

*   *   *

My father was reassigned to Ft. Myer, Virginia, just outside Washington in Arlington, during my mother's hospital stay. We remained there after she was released. Those were priceless days, filled with long walks at my mother's side. Often, we would walk amongst the graves in Arlington National Cemetery, and she would tell me of war and of the soldiering heroics of my father. There was wonderful time spent with him, too, and he taught me all sorts of marvelous things, including how to say the word "bullshit." My father thought the fact that his young son could say "bullshit" was hilarious, and he would take me around to his buddies on the post, and I would get to say "bullshit" ten or fifteen times before the visit was over.

One thing he did not tell me, however, was that there was a time to say "bullshit" and a time *not* to say "bullshit." One isn't born with that kind of knowledge. However, I soon did learn that one of the times it is absolutely mandatory not to say "bullshit" is when the chaplain has come to your house for a visit.

"Hi there, young man," said the chaplain as he entered our living room.

"Bullshit," said I.

After they had revived my mother and the chaplain had left, she instructed my father to take me into my bedroom and, to quote her, "teach this child never to say words like that again," which even I understood really meant, "beat this child senseless."

My father obviously felt a party to my indiscretion, so he devised a plan. He would strike the closet door with his belt, and I would scream out in pain with each lick.

"Wham!" went the belt against the door.

"Waaaaaa!" I cried out.

Three or four "whams" and "waaaas" later, we both got tickled and began to laugh. My mother opened the door. She tried to get the belt away from my father so she could render the punishment herself—to both of us. My parents wrestled playfully, and then they fell on my bed and I jumped in between them, and we all laughed ourselves silly. I think, in retrospect, that at that moment, I felt as much love as I have ever felt. On future occasions of spiritual revelry, it remained a comfort to think that perhaps some knowing, seeing power knew of the scarcity of our time left together and saw to it that we had such moments. If that is, indeed, the case, then blessed be He who provided them.

They remain my treasure.

*　　　　　*　　　　　*

My mother tried to explain Korea to me and why my father had to go there.

"Is that near heaven, Mama?" I asked her.

"No, son. Far from it," she said.

I didn't understand her explanation, of course, just as I had not understood when my father had tried to explain why my mother was going away.

All I knew was that one day my father took me into his arms and squeezed me, and he told me to take care of my mother, and then he stepped on another train, and he was gone. We were back on a train ourselves, my mother and I, in a few weeks. We took the Seaboard Silver Comet south. We would wait out the war with my grandparents, C. B. and Willie Word.

After their children all left Heard County and their health began to fail, C. B. and Willie also abandoned the family place and moved near their oldest daughter, Jessie, thirty miles away in Coweta County. They settled in a sleepy hamlet named Moreland, population three hundred, and likely that many dogs and twice as many chickens. C. B. bought twelve acres that sat behind the Baptist Church's cemetery and built himself a home there, and he busied himself keeping his acres in corn and potatoes, both sweet and Irish, and plum trees and scuppernong vines.

I missed my father during those days, but I was drawn ever closer to my mother. My spoiling was well under way. My grandfather, "Daddy Bun" to me, was the kind of man who attracted dogs and small children, so I spent a lot of time with him. He had little education, but he was a man of many talents, not the least of which were tossing a baseball to his four-year-old grandson, cutting off chickens' heads (the rest of which would be Sunday dinner), building homemade kites, catching fish, and shooting rabbits and squirrels.

We had a group prayer each night before we went to bed. Daddy Bun, Mama Willie, my mother, and I would gather in the tiny living room, drawing close to the kerosene stove that warmed the house. My grandfather would give thanks for rain, and then he would ask for the blessing of peace that would bring the boys back from Korea.

One night, my grandfather asked me to pray.

"What should I pray about, Daddy Bun?" I asked him.

"Pray your daddy is safe," he said.

I did.

The next day, I was with Daddy Bun in his fields. I asked him if God really heard prayers.

"He does," he said.

"Think my daddy's safe?" I asked.

"No way to know for certain, son," he said. "All we can do is keep praying."

*   *   *

My father was missing in action, the telegram said. His outfit had been surprised, and although his body had not been found, he was presumed dead with the rest of his comrades.

My mother drew me ever closer to her in those awful days after the telegram. I suppose any woman who thinks she has lost her man sees their child as a part of the husband, as a product of their love, and clings to that child for some sense of relief. I spent both days and nights at my mother's side. Often I would awaken to her sobbing into a pillow. At those times, I would hold her hand and twirl her hair between my fingers.

One miracle had saved my mother. I needed another to save my father. I got it. A second telegram arrived some weeks later, saying that he had been found, that he was alive, and that he would be coming home. My father called from Pearl Harbor on a Christmas Eve, and my mother cried again that night, too, but there is such a thing as sobbing happily, and I could tell the difference.

We were always getting on and off of trains in the early days of my life. Another one pulled into Atlanta's Union Station one afternoon, and my father stepped off. He was much thinner than I remembered him. We all hugged and we all cried some more, and then we sat and ate from a shoe box filled with fried chicken that Mama Willie had brought along.

We went back to Ft. Benning after that. He was a captain by then, and the Army had given him a soft job as the base athletic director. I would sit on his lap as he coached the basketball team, and it seemed like he had never gone away, and he told me he would never go away again.

"They've taken all the fight this soldier has," I remember his saying to my mother.

We built a house in Columbus, and I started school. There were more ball games, and we went to movies together, the three of us; and one summer my father packed up my mother and me and Daddy Bun and Mama

Willie, and we all went to Florida in our 1950 Hudson my father called the "Blue Goose." My father bought Daddy Bun some beer one night, and my grandfather drank a couple down and got a little high and began to hum, "What a Friend We Have in Jesus." Whenever my grandfather felt particularly happy, I had noticed, he would hum a few bars of "What a Friend We Have in Jesus." I never knew why.

My grandmother did not hold to drinking, however, not even a couple of beers on a Florida vacation. There is nothing so loud or fearsome, I would learn later, as a woman raging against the evils of alcohol, especially if her foursquare opposition to drink is built on a Biblical foundation. Mama Willie gave my grandfather one of the fiercest tongue-lashings my tender ears had ever heard, ending with the Biblical allusion, "A drunkard shall not enter the Kingdom of Heaven!" Daddy Bun just kept humming.

*   *   *

I first noticed something was wrong between my parents when they stopped sleeping in the same bed. My father moved into a third bedroom, and I would go first to his bed at night and he would tell me stories, and I would rub the back of his head and feel the shrapnel still lodged there. Then I would go into my mother's room and, often, I would catch her crying again. Sometimes, I would go to sleep beside her, still twirling her hair between my fingers.

Then there were arguments, most centered around my father's drinking, and he would be gone for days. When he came back, he would be unshaven and he would reek of a smell that was foreign to me. Then men in uniform began coming to our house to look for him, and my mother would tell them that he was ill.

He said strange things in those days. He talked about men he had seen die around him, and he would awaken us with screams in the night, and some nights he wouldn't even go to bed. He would sit at our kitchen table and pour an amber liquid out of a bottle into a glass, and then he would talk on the telephone for what seemed like hours, and he would be sobbing into it.

The day it ended, I was sitting in my desk in the first grade room at Rosemont Elementary School in Columbus.

It was springtime. Six weeks were left in my first school year. The door to my room had a window in it. That day, that last day, I looked up into the window in the door and I saw the Army insignia on my father's hat. He walked into my room in the middle of class, whispered something to my teacher, and then motioned for me to come with him.

When we were in the car, he told me that my mother had gone to visit Daddy Bun and Mama Willie for a few days, and that he and I were going on a trip.

He had a bag packed for me. We drove to Atlanta and we boarded another train. We stopped in some strange place called Columbia, South Carolina, and stayed in a motel for several days. My father, I noticed, was no longer wearing his uniform.

After that, we caught another train, and we visited relatives I had never seen before in another town I had never seen before, Savannah. I hadn't talked to my mother in more than a week.

"Is Mama coming to see us?" I would ask.

"Soon," said my father.

Another week, and then we were on a third train, this time to Portsmouth, Virginia, where there were more relatives. My father never went outside the house very much in Portsmouth, and when he did go out, it was only at night. I still hadn't heard from my mother. I missed her.

My father had gone AWOL, I discovered later. Thirteen years of service were going down the drain. The man had been through two wars. He had Purple Hearts and a Bronze Star, but the strain of two wars had been too much, and then the drinking had started and the arguments had followed.

So one day when my mother had gone off to work, my father had hit the air and had taken me with him.

My mother was frantic when she got out of the car in front of the house where we were staying in Portsmouth. She had gone to my Uncle Frank, the lawyer, and he had tracked us from Atlanta to Columbia and then to Savannah and then to Virginia, and he had driven my mother to Portsmouth to get me.

What was happening? Why all the loud voices? I was happy to have both my parents again, but I didn't have them as I wanted them. They were enemies.

"Mama," I asked, "why are you and Daddy fighting?"

"He's sick, son," she answered me. "Your daddy is very sick, and you have to go with me so that he can get well."

We drove all night back to Atlanta in my Uncle Frank's car, and since there was no other option—my mother couldn't hold the house in Columbus on a teacher's pay—

we went back to the little house in Moreland, back to live with Daddy Bun and Mama Willie.

They drummed my father out of the Army as unfit to continue, and he set to roaming and drinking more and more. I would see him only occasionally after that, but each time he would promise that someday soon, he would come tapping on the window outside the room where my mother and I slept, and he would say, "Christine, Christine. . . . I've come to get you and my son," and we would leave and be together again. And I would ask, "For always, Daddy?" and he would answer, "For always."

I listened for his voice night after night, and I lived on the hope that one night I would hear it. But it never came.

Sometimes at night, when I didn't do it on my own, my mother would ask me to hold her hand and twirl her hair between my fingers.

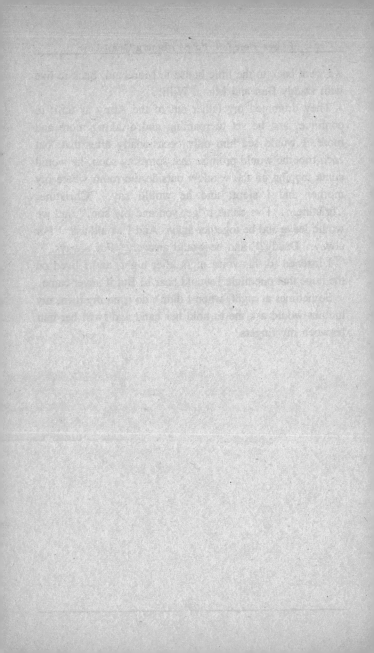

III

Never Kiss a Lady
When Her Mouth
Is Full of Snuff

A S I LOOK back on it, I suppose my mother really
didn't know any better.

After we moved back to live with my grandparents in
Moreland the second time, I started second grade in the
little elementary school there. The students were a bit
different from those I had encountered my first-grade year
in the relative metropolis of Columbus. Moreland's was a
country school, drawing the sons and daughters of
pulpwooders, sheet rockers, sawmill hands, and sharecrop-
pers. I had traveled some by then, although I was still only
six, but I had never seen anything quite like the group that
assembled the first day of classes in Moreland. There were
the Garfield brothers, for instance, a rather disagreeable
threesome who seemed to take a certain joy in raising large
knots on the heads of their classmates. They brought a

homemade explosive device made from gunpowder to school the first day and blew out all the windows in the third-grade room.

My instincts told me right away that the Garfields were not to be messed with. I tried to explain that fact of life to my mother the next morning, when she insisted that I wear short pants to school, but she wouldn't listen. So off to school I went with my knees exposed, knowing that if the Garfields spotted me in that outfit, I likely would not live out the day. I was nearly correct in my assumption.

I managed to avoid them all morning, but then came the dreaded recess. The Garfield brothers—Frankie, whose nickname was deservedly "Dynamite," Harold, and Dickie— spotted me and my shorts, as I attempted to hide behind the monkey bars on the playground.

"What's your name, fancy pants?" asked Frankie, the oldest, who was in the seventh grade.

I was barely able to speak from the fear and trembling. I managed to get out a feeble, "Lewis." I thought of perhaps offering them my first year's salary when I got out of college to spare me, but things were moving too quickly.

"Your mama put them short pants on you?" asked Harold, a fifth-grader who was already the size of a Plymouth.

I promised to bring a written note from my mother the next day, in which she would explain to the Garfields how I had resisted the short pants, with an addendum promising I would never show up at school in such an outfit again, if it so offended them.

"You want me to whoop him, Frankie?" the youngest Garfield, Dickie, a third-grader, asked his older brother. "Or you want to do it?"

I stood frozen in fear, awaiting Frankie's answer. I did feel some better about the situation at this point, however, and made a mental note to thank the Garfields later for deciding to designate only one of their lot to raise knots on my head, rather than all three taking turns.

Suddenly, something happened that assured me there was, indeed, a God who watched over each of his sparrows, especially if they happened to be wearing short pants. Before the Garfields could decide which one of them was going to welcome me to Moreland School, Arnold Bates, who was a teacher's pet because he was always answering questions first and never doing anything to antagonize his instructors—such as making obscene figures out of the modeling clay or tearing out pages from his reading book to make spitballs—walked past us, eating a Hollywood candy bar.

The Garfields were poor children, who never had money for candy of their own. Later I would learn that each had a voracious sweet tooth, however, and they satisfied their desire for candy by taking it away from the younger, smaller children on the playground. They left me with my knees knocking in my short pants and chased down Arnold Bates, took his Hollywood candy bar away from him, and gave him a few lumps on the head while they were at it.

When I returned home from classes, I explained to my mother how I had barely escaped being maimed by the Garfields because of my short pants, and, because she was a wonderful, understanding person who didn't have any children to spare, she promised me I would not be forced to return to school similarly attired.

The first year we were back with my grandparents in Moreland, my mother found a job teaching first grade in another county school, fifteen miles away. She would be making one hundred and twenty dollars a month, a paltry sum even for 1953.

She bought a 1948 Chevrolet in which to travel back and forth, and we lived on a tight budget. Still, I wanted for very little. Daddy Bun maintained his six acres and a yard-full of chickens, and Mama Willie kept our table loaded.

My grandmother cooked her cornbread in a rectangular pan, which provided two crusty, delicious end pieces. We bought homemade butter from a man who owned a dairy, and to this day I have tasted very little of anything that was better than one of those end pieces from my grandmother's cornbread, lavished with a hunk of home-made butter.

There were only two bedrooms in my grandparents' house. They slept in one. I bunked with my mother in the other. We had no television. Our evenings were spent quietly in the living room together. My grandfather taught me the rules of Rook, and we spent many hours playing cards on the living room floor.

Besides tending to his fields, my grandfather also had part-time work at the little Atlanta and West Point R.R. shack, and he was also the janitor at my school. Rather than being embarrassed by that fact, I was quite proud. "Mr. Word," they called him at school, and he was up each morning before dawn, loading the stoves in each room with coal. He would leave the school after the fires were built and go to work at the railroad shack. He would return in the afternoon to clean the school, and then he would go home and work his crops.

He was a totally unpretentious man who had known little more than hard work his entire life. When I reached the third grade at Moreland School, a new principal arrived. I was standing next to my grandfather when the new principal introduced himself.

"You must be Mr. Word, the custodian I've heard so much about," he said.

"No, sir," answered my grandfather, "I ain't nobody but the janitor."

I looked forward to the summer after second grade. I had managed to stay out of the Garfields' way the entire year, and I had met and made some new friends, Danny and Bobby and Mike and Dudley. I was beginning to enjoy living in the little village. Adventure awaited at every turn.

I could go fishing or blackberry-picking with my grandfather. There were always dogs around. There were creeks to dam and trees to climb and mules to ride.

My summer was not to be one of contentment, however. It seemed to me that every time I relaxed in the knowledge there would be no further disruptions in my life, one would jump up out of nowhere.

My mother broke the news to me as best she could. She took me into her arms and told me that in order to make more money as a teacher, it would be necessary for her to attend school in the summertime, and that she would have to go and live with my Uncle Johnny, the doctor, during the weekdays.

"I will be home every Friday," she said. "Daddy Bun and Mama Willie will take good care of you while I'm gone."

I was devastated by the news. I recalled those days without her when she was in the hospital, and then my father had gone away to Korea and then he had come back, only to leave again. For good. I remembered being away from her the summer before, when my father had taken me to Virginia.

My Uncle Johnny lived in Tallapoosa, Georgia, which was near Carrollton, the home of West Georgia College, where my mother planned to attend classes to obtain further certification as a teacher.

The old Chevrolet was barely functional after a year's driving her back and forth to school, so I walked hand-to-hand with my mother from my grandparents' house up to the highway, where she would flag down the Greyhound.

I prayed the bus would never come over the hill, but soon I saw its snarling face. Daddy Bun picked me up and held me as the bus drove away, carrying my mother.

That summer was an awful one, save those wonderful Friday evenings when I waited next to the highway for the bus which would bring my mother home for the weekends.

Sunday nights, however, were long and lonesome. I was getting my first taste of what anguish there is to love a woman and then have her leave me. After my mother had left again on Sunday nights, I would sit on the front porch with Daddy Bun. I would put my head in his lap. We would listen for the evening mail train, bound for Montgomery, and the dogs would come around. Mama Willie might even bring us out a piece of blackberry pie, made from the berries we had picked, but none of that could fill the void left by my mother's absence.

I missed her most at night, when things made noises outside, when the walls cracked, when the old clock in the kitchen first grinded and then gonged out the hours. Mondays were agonizingly slow. Tuesdays weren't much better. There was some hope on Wednesdays. Thursdays I began to feel better, and Fridays, oh, Fridays! The bus would arrive at six, but I usually was waiting at the side of the highway by four. When my mother stepped off the bus, I would fling myself into her arms, and nothing ever felt as good as that first, wonderful squeeze, when I realized she would be with me, next to me, for the entire weekend.

I would sit with her as she studied her books, and I suppose even then I felt a certain admiration for her. She bore me late in life, at thirty-five. She was already into her early forties, and she had seen her husband off to two wars, and thought him dead in the second.

He had come back to her that second time, too, but not the same man she had known. She lived through his drinking and his depression, only to see both get worse. And then she saw their relationship fall completely away, and she had to give up her life with him to start over, struggling to right herself.

When she came home for good that long, first summer in Moreland, I was thrilled. And there was even more good news: No longer would she be teaching at another school. The first-grade teaching position in Moreland had opened, and she was to fill it. The first morning of classes, we walked to school together. She went to the first-grade classroom, and I went to the third. There would be some disadvantages to having my mother on the faculty. My teachers somehow expected more of me, and they could alert her very quickly if I behaved in a manner not befitting a teacher's son. However, there was one distinct advantage. When, and if, the Garfields ever got around to making me pay for the fact that I had dared wear short pants to school, my mother would be close by to nurse my wounds.

I learned a lot in the third grade. As I look back upon it, I received an excellent education from all my teachers—all women. A woman taught me how to read and how to count, and what the average annual rainfall is in Ethiopia. One of the most important lessons I learned was never to dance with a girl twice my size.

A couple of times each week, we had music class in the third grade. Sometimes we played our tonettes, small wind instruments that were nothing more than glorified kazoos. By the Christmas break, my class could serenade itself with tonette renditions of both "Twinkle, Twinkle Little Star" and "Up on the Housetop," in keeping with the season at hand.

Other times, we would all be given an instrument, and we would play along with a record in Mrs. Evans' Third-Grade Rhythm Band.

A number of instruments make up a rhythm band. The more gifted children got tamborines. Others played the triangle or shook the shaker, a dried gourd with tiny seeds inside it. I, however, was always a stick player. Unfortunately, I had not inherited any of my father's musical talents, and once Mrs. Evans determined I had all the rhythm of a pulpwood truck being cranked on a cold morning, I was stuck with the sticks forever.

Playing sticks required little or no talent whatsoever. As a matter of fact, all you had to do was bang one stick onto the other in time with the music, which sounds relatively simple. For me, it wasn't. I was always about a halfbeat off and occasionally even dropped one of my sticks, a further testament not only to my lack of musical abilities, but also to my lack of manual dexterity.

However, I much preferred a morning of being banished to sticks over the times Mrs. Evans decided to teach us folk dances. The "Hokey-Pokey" was big in those days. You stick your big foot in, you stick your big foot out, you stick your big foot in, and you shake it all about.

That, I could handle. It was the "Virginia Reel" that was a problem, because by that time, Alice McTavish, who was as big as a Garfield boy and nearly as mean, had taken somewhat of a liking to me, a fact that caused me much embarrassment in front of my friends.

Worse, whenever it would come my turn to take Alice for a spin down the line when we were doing the Reel, she insisted upon leading and did so with incredible strength for an eight-year-old girl. She had a huge head that was square, and so was the rest of her body. Ray Nitchske, the all-Pro Green Bay Packers linebacker, probably looked a lot like Alice McTavish when he was eight.

Alice would crush me with her gigantic arms and spin

me around with incredible speed. How I avoided serious whiplash is still a puzzle, but I always would be quite dizzy after dancing with Alice, and once I even threw up on her. She promptly bounced a couple of knuckles off the top of my head.

I thought perhaps that incident would convince Alice to offer her flirtations to someone with a stronger stomach, but it didn't. She insisted upon sitting behind me in class, and she took great sport in crashing her palms around my ears, which caused a severe ringing sound in my head and made it impossible to listen when Mrs. Evans was explaining the multiplication tables. I still have trouble multiplying anything more complicated than three-times-three because of all this.

I tried throwing up on Alice a couple of more times in order to put an end to her advances, but the only way I was ever able to stifle her interest in me was to offer Dickie Garfield a Hollywood candy bar to threaten to beat her up if she ever came near me again.

Dickie and Alice finally did come to blows over the issue, but Dickie was so enraptured by a girl who could actually go several rounds with him, he forgot about the Hollywood bar, and they were nearly inseparable after that. I hear they later married and made quite a good livelihood for themselves as a mixed doubles tag-team wrestling duo.

When I was in the fourth grade, they closed the old frame Moreland School, your basic firetrap, and built a new one of brick, which included a new cafeteria. The food at Moreland School was never exactly *haute cuisine*. On Mondays we had hot dogs, and rice pudding for dessert. On Tuesdays we had what was loosely referred to as meat loaf, and rice pudding for dessert. Wednesdays was some sort of brown mystery meat, with gravy on top of it, and rice pudding for dessert. Thursdays we ate chipped beef on toast, that likely was left over from the Spanish-American War, with rice pudding for dessert. And because there was one Catholic family in school, I suppose, we had fish sticks on Fridays, and rice pudding for dessert. Occasionally, I still have nightmares in which I am surrounded by giant globs of rice pudding.

There was, however, one spectacular offering in the school cafeteria, and that was Mrs. Murphy's rolls. I did not realize it at the time, but I would come to admire greatly any woman empowered with the ability to cook good things to eat, and any woman so blessed who would practice her art without the slightest bit of assistance on my part—as in, "Honey, I have just cooked up a big apple pie. Why don't you just sit there and let me bring you a hot slice. And would you like some ice cream on the top?"

I would, in fact, run into women later in life who had absolutely no idea of how to cook, and even if they had, they would have wanted to cook fancy dishes I had no interest in.

I am convinced there is a special place in heaven for women who have labored in the kitchen during their lifetimes. This includes mothers and wives and ladies who run diners, and even waitresses at Krystal hamburger places, who don't have many teeth and pronounce "Krystal" as "Kris-chial." The Lord probably likes some of those little bite-sized burgers occasionally, too.

Mrs. Murphy was a tiny, sweet woman who was in charge of the school kitchen, and at least three times a week, she would cook up a batch of homemade rolls.

My classmates generally were divided into two groups in those days—those whose parents could afford the twenty cents a day for lunch money, and those whose parents couldn't. In fact, the social lines between students were drawn in just that fashion. The "pays" felt somewhat superior to "frees," poor children who lived in shacks out in the country, who rarely had shoes to wear, whose personal hygiene was suspect, and whose appetites never waned. You could tell where a "free" had sat in the cafeteria after lunch. His or her plate would be completely empty. Even the rice pudding would be gone.

We also lined up in the classroom to go to lunch each day as "pays" and "frees." The pays were allowed to go first. We marched through the line and got our trays and our glasses of milk, while the frees had to stand outside and wait until we were served.

I'm not certain whose idea that was, but the segregation of the two groups did work in favor of the pays—we got the freshest and the hottest of Mrs. Murphy's rolls, and since they put all the milk out at once, we got the glasses that were still cold.

When the frees walked through the line, only the dregs were normally left in the roll bin, and their milk was warm.

Not yet old enough to understand the full impact poverty could have on a group of individuals, I passed off all this as my good fortune and the second group's bad luck.

Mrs. Murphy, however, did take notice of the inconsistency of how her youthful customers were being served, and she also took notice of the fact that those who received free lunches seemed to be a much hungrier lot and therefore much more appreciative of her daily offerings.

The pays continued to go first through the cafeteria line, but Mrs. Murphy, bless her heart, held back some of the bigger, softer rolls for those poor souls waiting in arrears. She also instituted a policy whereby each student drew his own milk from the dispenser, so every student would have a glass of milk that was fresh and cold.

We pays grumbled a bit over the fact that we no longer got the pick of Mrs. Murphy's rolls, but the frees took it as a personal favor. One day, one of the frees came to school accompanied by his father, a sawmill hand who came to see the "roll lady."

"I got four other young'uns at home, ma'am," the man said to Mrs. Murphy. "If it would be all right, could my boy here bring his rolls home one day so they could have some?"

The man left with a huge sack filled with Mrs. Murphy's rolls that day, and I think I noticed her eyes were red when she served my plate at lunchtime.

*   *   *

My mother had saved enough money to buy a new car the summer after my fourth-grade year, and she was able to commute back and forth to her summer classes on a daily basis. No longer did I have to spend those agonizing weeks away from her.

While she was away attending classes each day, however, my grandmother, Mama Willie, took it upon herself to begin my religious instruction. Daddy Bun, turned off by the modern ways of the church—educated preachers who read their sermons from prepared notes, and the demise of foot-washing—no longer attended formal services. But he did remain a rock-hard believer, and once he chased a group of Jehovah's Witnesses away from our door with a shotgun, because he did not believe their teachings and beliefs were consistent with his. That, and the fact they drove up in an expensive-looking car. Had they arrived in a horse-drawn wagon or in an older model automobile, he still likely would have turned them away, but he probably would have been at least tolerant enough to have kept his shotgun in the closet.

My grandmother, however, had maintained her ties with formal religion in the little Baptist Church across from her house, and she read the Bible daily and listened to all sorts of radio preachers trying to drive out the devil through the airwaves. Every Sunday morning I was awakened by the "Gospel Music Jubilee" playing on the radio.

Mama Willie's beliefs were fundamental. You did exactly what the Good Book said, or you burned in hell.

My mother was never one to discipline me. I suppose she couldn't bring herself to give me a pounding, even when I deserved it, after some of the things we had been through together.

Mama Willie, however, was never one to spare the rod, and she had a number of devious ways to punish a child. She had learned these methods from her own strict father and from raising five children. Grandmothers, I have surmised, usually have two sides to them. One side dotes and pampers. The other side would have made a good Marine drill instructor.

Mama Willie's favorite method of punishment was to deliver a harsh switching upon the backs of the legs of her victim. There was more to it than that, however. When she had decided it was time I learned a lesson for unruly behavior, she would send me to fetch the object she would use to administer the pain.

"Go out," she would say, "and fetch me a keen hickory switch." This was akin to asking the guest of honor at an execution to furnish the rope for his hanging.

I was no dummy. The first time Mama Willie told me to go out and bring her a switch so she could whip me with it, I came back with a twig, which was a horrible mistake.

"Young man," she sneered at me, "you go back outside and bring me something I can switch you with, or I'm going outside and cut one myself, and I'm going to see to it you don't stop hurting for a week."

I came back this time with an appropriate tool and took seven or eight stinging blows to the backs of my legs. It is a natural reflex, when one is being flogged on the backs of one's legs with a switch, to attempt to cover the area taking the punishment with one's hands.

My grandmother was wise to that, too.

"You keep your hands by your side," she would say, "or I'm going to whip you until you do."

I tried everything to get away from my grandmother's punishment, including a futile attempt to bolt from her grasp and run to Alabama and make a new life for myself there. She was a strong woman, however, and her hold on me was unbreakable.

I also tried to show my deep regret for my transgression, promising never to hold my bowl of soup to my mouth and make motorboat sounds in it again, for instance.

"Please stop, Mama Willie!" I would beseech her. "I won't ever do it again, I promise!"

If I pleaded long enough and loudly enough, it did seem to have some effect. It was at this point that I developed my "I-promise-never-to-do-it-again" technique that I would use with other enraged women whom I would confront as the years passed.

My grandmother had an even more treacherous means of dishing out punishment, however. That was her "promise whippings."

Let's say I complained about a third-water bath in the morning. The well was always low in the summertime, and in an effort to conserve water, people in those days often bathed in the same water. First one up got first water, second one second, etc. Because other members of the household were usually up and at whatever their task before me, I often got stuck with hand-me-down bath water.

"Did you take a bath this morning, young man?" my grandmother would ask me.

"The water was too dirty," I would reply. "There were a lot of strange things floating in it."

"Don't you know the well is low?" she would continue.

"I don't care," I would sass her back. "I'm not taking a bath in that water. It's green."

"Are you disputing my word?" Mama Willie would ask me, her voice rising in anger.

It was either go take a bath in the green water, or face a

whipping. There were times when I chose corporal punishment over a bath in green water with strange things floating in it. For such capital offenses, my grandmother would go to the promise-whipping, which worked this way:

"I'm not going to whip you right now," she would say. "I want you to think about what you have done all day. I want you to think about how you have sassed me and talked back to me, and when you come home from school this afternoon, I am going to wear the filling out of you."

Imagine, if you will, this poor child sitting in class, attempting to learn the difference between quotients and divisors, knowing that with every tick of the clock he was one step closer to having his hindparts beaten red and raw by his grandmother.

I, however, did devise another means of either escaping my punishment altogether, or at least having it reduced somewhat.

My grandmother was one of the all-time snuff-dippers. As she pored over her Bible each day, she would load up her bottom lip with a generous dip and rock gently and contentedly with the Word of the Lord and the best the Bruton's Snuff Company had to offer.

On my way home from school on those days I had been promised a whipping, I would occasionally spend the dime my mother had given me for an after-school treat on a small ten-cent tin of Bruton's, that was always in stock at Cureton and Cole's store.

Either Mr. J. W. Thompson or Mr. Lee Evans, who owned the store and worked in it, would sell me the snuff. They thought it strange that a nine-year-old boy already had developed a taste for snuff, but when I told them it was a gift for my grandmother, they were more than happy to sell it to me.

"You must be a mighty nice young man to be spending your candy money on a can of snuff for your grandmother," one of the men would say to me.

I took the compliment and never told anyone that the real reason I was blowing perfectly good candy money on snuff, was that it was a last-ditch attempt to avoid a beating with a peace offering

My grandmother was, in fact, touched by my sacrifice, and normally would let me off with nothing more than a tongue-lashing. Thus, I learned another lesson that would be invaluable in subsequent dealings with women—you occasionally can buy off one with a gift.

Mama Willie would insist that I spend at least a half-hour each day sitting next to her while she read the Bible to me. She also told me stories of how Christ had been born, and how he had been crucified, and how one day, on that great gettin' up morning, he was going to return.

Her house, as I mentioned, sat directly behind the Baptist cemetery. In fact, my grandfather grew onions on the adjoining property to the cemetery, and we called his subsequent yield, "graveyard onions."

The cemetery, however, was a great source of fear for me, especially after my grandmother read to me from Revelation and then informed me that upon Christ's return, there would be a loud blast of Gabriel's trumpet, followed by Christ's judgment of the quick and the dead. She further informed me that all the graves would open and spew forth their holdings.

"Let me see if I have this straight," I said to my grandmother. "When Gabriel blows his horn and Jesus comes down out of the sky, the graves out in the cemetery are going to open up, and the people that are in there are going to come out?"

"That's exactly right," said my grandmother.

Afterwards I would lie in my bed at night and look out my window at the cemetery, and wait nervously for a trumpet's blast, and for the earth to tremble, and for those graves suddenly to open and bring forth who-knows-what.

One evening, a group of Boy Scouts was helping the men cook the pigs for the annual Moreland Fourth of July Barbecue at the Masonic Lodge, which was located just to the other side of the cemetery, across the highway that adjoined it. As I lay in my bed, pondering the Rapture, one of the Boy Scouts pulled out his bugle and played "Taps," a tune with which I was unfamiliar at the time.

I bolted out of my bed and ran for my grandmother.

"Mama Willie! Mama Willie!" I screamed. "It's Gabriel, and he's over at the Masonic Lodge blowing his trumpet!"

Next, I fully expected to see the marble gravestones in the cemetery crack open and to be face-to-face with Jesus in a matter of seconds. I hoped he had failed to notice the fact that I had recently lied to my grandmother about who went into her refrigerator and ate the rest of the banana pudding she was saving for lunch. I had taken it into a hall closet to eat it. Maybe Jesus was too busy planning his comeback to have seen me, I thought.

Mama Willie quickly indicated it was a false alarm, but she was impressed with the fact that I had taken the Second Coming seriously, and she promised to make me a new banana pudding the next day, since somebody, probably Daddy Bun, had deprived me the day before.

I still didn't have the courage to confess what I had done, and chalked up yet one more sin I would have to answer to when the Judgment Day finally did arrive.

I worried about going to hell a lot in those days, too, and here again it was my God-fearing grandmother who instilled that concern in me. We burned our garbage out in a distant field. It was usually my job to help my grandmother carry the family refuse out to the burning site.

One day, as we stood together watching the fire melt away the eggshells and the cantaloupe rinds and whatever else had been discarded, she said to me, "Go put your hands next to the fire and feel how hot it is."

I did that, and then she said, "The fires in hell will be a million times hotter. You remember that the next time you tell me you didn't eat the banana pudding when you did."

She was wise, this woman, and I was careful after that always to tell her the truth. The incident had another lasting effect on me, too. To this day, whenever I see a garbage truck or smell burning eggshells or cantaloupe rinds, I feel the hot breath of the devil on my neck.

I do not wish to imply my grandmother was without tenderness or affection, however. She simply was the family enforcer. But she was also quick to listen to my problems, and as quick to praise me when I was good as she was to switch the tar out of me when I was bad.

My grandmother also enjoyed kissing her grandchildren, which wouldn't have been all that much of a problem, had it not been for her aforementioned taste for snuff.

Snuff has a pungent aroma that will burn your nose and

eyes. When one is kissed by a person who is dipping snuff, it causes the kissee to sneeze and cough and want to run outside for a whiff of fresh air. I really don't know how my grandfather stood it all those years, for he must have led the league in getting snuff-kissed. I don't recall ever having to kiss any other woman with her mouth full of snuff besides my grandmother, but I did later meet a man whose wife chewed tobacco.

"How do you stand it?" I asked him.

"It's not so bad," he replied. "Besides, when she's holding a big plug in her mouth, she doesn't try to say very much, because as soon as she opens her mouth, she has to spit."

*   *   *

By the time I began the fifth grade, I had begun to feel some sense of security again. I had my mother and my grandmother and my grandfather, and we all lived together in that tiny house near the cemetery, and I had firmly entrenched myself in the little community. I was a Cub Scout, and attended Methodist Youth Fellowship on Sunday nights, and rode bikes, and threw rocks at road signs with my friends, and had a good dog, and one of the Garfields had moved on to the high school in the county seat, which cut down on my odds of being brutalized on the school grounds.

My mother, as well, had settled into the routine of life in Moreland. We still heard from my father every now and then, and once we slipped away to meet him for a weekend in Atlanta. Daddy Bun and Mama Willie were not at all anxious to see their daughter take up with the man who had hurt her so much. My mother said we were merely going to visit some of her old friends.

It was nice to walk in between them again, as we strolled down the city streets one evening, window shopping after a Joan Crawford movie. My father always enjoyed Joan Crawford movies.

But I could tell the visit was nothing more than just that. He would not come to the window one night and take us away. I loved him very much, but I also had become very protective of my mother, and I remembered her tearful nights. I was content, by that time, to leave things as they were.

Occasional visits with my father were marvelous. Despite his problems, he could still laugh a lot and still find ways to make those around him do the same. He still told the stories, still found an old piano to tear apart occasionally, and, perhaps out of guilt, he sent me home after each visit loaded with toys and gifts.

I had trouble keeping up with his whereabouts, however. He had problems holding a job. He borrowed money from friends, he wrote bad checks, he moved in to one place, and then he moved out one night and never left a forwarding address.

So be it, I said to myself. He will turn up again sooner or later, and in the meantime, I had my mother. She would never have to go away again, and we were growing ever the more close. She was honest with me. She encouraged me. Except for a brief moment of grossly overestimating my abilities by enrolling me in piano lessons (that lasted only until my teacher threw up her hands in disgust and suggested I couldn't beat a tamborine because it took both hands—something I already knew from my rhythm band days), my mother seemed to understand me.

But there was something I had failed to understand about her. She was still basically a young woman, with the needs and desires of same. Although she had not yet officially divorced my father, she, too, knew there was no hope for reconciliation. Yet, stuck in small-town Georgia, a first-grade schoolteacher with a ten-year-old son, living with her parents, she obviously yearned for companionship. And when it finally was offered to her, I did all that was in my power to keep the intruder out.

IV

My Mother Loves Me, This I Know, 'Cause Hand-Squoze Orange Juice Tells Me So

H ERBERT BERN ATKINSON—he went by "H.B."
—was born in coastal South Carolina, a member of a large family that saw its living grow out of the black, sandy dirt in the form of tobacco plants.

He, too, was called away for World War II. He returned home to South Carolina and married. His wife died young of cancer, however, and so he set off to traveling. He wound up in Newnan, Georgia, county seat of Coweta, and took to selling appliances. Enough background.

My Aunt Una and her husband came to visit my mother and me and my grandfather and grandmother for a week, and one evening they suggested to my mother that she needed to get out of the house. They took her to the Veteran's Club in Newnan, which, unless one happened to be a member of the local landed gentry with enough money for country club dues, was the only spot in town offering any semblance to night life that wasn't likely to be accompanied by at least one beer-bottle fight and a couple of cuttings.

H.B. was only in his mid-thirties, younger than my mother. He was at the Veteran's Club the night the two Word girls from Heard County walked in with Una's husband as their escort.

The small number of available women in such a tiny populace would make any man desperate. You can sell washing machines and refrigerators for just so long before it becomes absolutely necessary to find relief in the form of feminine companionship.

H.B. watched Una and Christine and tried to decide which one was with the man who had accompanied them. He put his money on Christine, walked over to where she was sitting, and said, "This doesn't look very even. Mind if I join you?"

Christine—it had been a long time—was unsure; but Una, the ever-affable, ever-fun-loving Una, invited him to join the group. I, meanwhile, was home in bed in my grandparents' house, with one ear tuned to Gabriel, as usual, and the other tuned to the sound of my uncle's car coming back into the driveway.

What could be taking them so long, I wondered? What was this Veteran's Club? I had never trusted Una's husband, my Uncle John, in the first place. He was always tweeking my ears and pulling on my nose. Every child, I suppose, has at least one uncle who is always tweeking his ears and pulling on his nose. This was all Uncle John's fault, I figured. He had convinced my mother to go out, and they were all having a good time, and here I was lonesome and afraid and quite angry that I had not been included in the plans.

When I had lived with both of my parents, they had rarely left me at home. I had been an Officer's Club regular by the time I was three, which is also when I started drinking beer. When the table got up to dance, I took a practice sip out of everybody's beer glass and found the golden brew quite to my liking.

They're probably drinking beer, I thought to myself, fighting back the tears. At midnight, I was still awake, listening for a car in the driveway. Is there anything more lonely than listening for a car in the driveway? When finally I heard my Uncle John's car, I jumped out of bed and rushed to the front door and awaited their arrival. Sure enough, I smelled beer on my mother's breath. In my best evangelical voice I had picked up from listening to radio preachers with my grandmother, I reminded all three of the backsliders, ''A drunkard shall not enter the Kingdom of Heaven!''

My mother had never threatened me with physical violence before, but she suggested that if I were not back in bed in the next three seconds, four tops, she would beat me within an inch of my life.

The next day, H.B. was all they could talk about.

''Your mother met herself a boyfriend last night,'' chided my Uncle John.

''They have a date tonight, too,'' said my Aunt Una. ''Isn't that exciting?''

About as exciting as dancing with Alice McTavish, I thought.

The pangs of fear and jealousy were fierce. Who was this H.B. person, and what was he doing messing around my mother? This was my first episode of jealousy. (Unfortunately, it would not be my last.) It was an odd feeling, a terrible feeling. It made my stomach hurt and it made me dizzy. I wanted to cry. I wanted to lash out at someone. I thought of calling my father. He would put a stop to this nonsense. But the last I heard of him, he was in Mississippi someplace with a carnival that was heading west.

I confronted my mother.

"He's a nice man," she said.

"I don't care," I replied, fighting back the tears.

My mother had a way of explaining things to me. She would kneel down, look me squarely in the face, look into my eyes and smile, and when she was finished talking to me, she would draw me near her and I would understand.

But not this time.

"Tell him I hate him," I said.

"I can't do that," said my mother. "You'll like him. I want you to meet him tonight when he comes to get me."

Two nights in a row! Two nights in a row I would be left at home without my mother.

When the dreaded H.B. arrived, I hid under the bed. I likely would still be there, had my grandmother not taken a broom and flushed me out as if I were the dog.

I wouldn't shake H.B.'s hand when he offered it to me. I wouldn't speak, and I buried my face in my hands so that I wouldn't have to look at him. For once in my life, I wished my mother dipped snuff. That would keep him away from her.

They married at the Moreland Methodist Church five days after my tenth birthday. My grandfather wouldn't go to the ceremonies, so they asked me to give the bride away. That likely was my grandmother's idea, what with her fiendish insistence that when somebody was going to get punished, they take an integral part in the arrangements.

I said my lines perfectly, albeit *sotto voce*. After a week's honeymoon, they came back to my grandparents' house, where we would live until a new home could be built a few hundred yards away on acreage that previously had served as a cornfield.

I figured that with a new husband, my mother wouldn't have as much time for me, and I could sense that this man was a strict disciplinarian with some rather strong ideas about children helping out around the house. I had a few chores, but nothing so time-consuming that it would take me away from such activities as goofing off with my friends, or standing in the driveway batting rocks with a broomstick, replaying the entire 1955 Brooklyn Dodgers schedule in my mind.

The one possibility I didn't consider, however, was how sleeping arrangements might change with a fifth body moving into our two-bedroom household. My mother and I had always shared a bed, if for no other reason, because there were only two beds in the house.

I figured H.B. for a pallet on the floor. Imagine my surprise the first night they were back from their honeymoon. I began to get a bit suspicious when H.B. took his bags into *my* bedroom, and began to hang his clothes in *my* closet. Then I noticed my mother putting covers on the sofa in the living room.

I couldn't bring myself to ask directly who the covers on the sofa were for.

"Sofa's a little short for a bed, isn't it?" I asked my mother.

"I think it will do fine, son," she answered.

"Well," I continued, "it might do fine for, say, a little boy, but I think a large person, like a man, might be a little uncomfortable sleeping there."

My mother caught on to my concern. She finished making up the bed on the sofa and said to me, "H.B. and I are married now. That means we will be sleeping together."

"And that means I'm going to sleep on the so—" I stammered.

"Yes, it does," my mother interrupted me.

"What if I get scared or sick in the night?" I asked as the tears welled in my eyes.

"I will be only a few feet away from you," my mother answered.

I knew there was no reason to take the argument any further. I knew I was the odd-child-out in the flip for the bed. I clung, however, to one final straw.

"Will you not close the door?" I asked, my voice and eyes pleading for agreement on at least this minor point.

"You will have to ask H.B. about that," my mother answered me.

When H.B. shut the door to their bedroom, I died a thousand deaths. I was livid with anger and rage. There I was, abandoned to a sofa in the living room like an unwanted waif, and then they had the audacity to shut the door, as if something were going on inside that they didn't want me to know about.

I banged on their door at planned intervals for weeks after that, feigning every illness from the mumps to a change in a wart or a mole. I pretended to hear noises, I pretended to see things moving about in the room. Sometimes, I banged on the door just to tell H.B. and my mother something humorous a friend of mine had done at school the previous day.

H.B. took it for awhile, and then he instructed me that if I ever banged on the door again, the house had better be on fire. I strongly considered arson after that. It hadn't been mentioned in the Ten Commandments, so I figured it would be an easy enough sin to get forgiveness for. And maybe while H.B. jumped up to help fight the fire, I could run get into bed with my mother.

When we finally moved into the new house and I got my own room and my own radio, things improved in that area, however. Besides, I was eleven by then, a little old to be sleeping with my mother.

I still hadn't exactly warmed to H.B., however. He was much quieter than my father, he had little or no interest in sports, and my worst fears had come true concerning his feelings about children and the work ethic.

"When I was your age," he would say to me, "I was chopping tobacco ten hours a day."

I was not impressed, however, and I had decided by that time that anything to do with any manner of agriculture was not for me. Pulling corn I had found to be a difficult and monotonous task, and picking up potatoes and putting them into a bucket, while somebody plowed the row in front of you, was even more difficult. Five or six potatoes in a bucket makes a heavy load, and the potatoes won't jump into the bucket. You have to bend down and pick them up.

The only work around the house I really enjoyed was sitting with my mother and shelling butter beans and peas. She had surprisingly remained a good and anxious listener, despite the fact that she had a husband around. She surprised me on a number of other fronts, too. Rather than becoming less interested in me, she had become even more willing to spend time with me, whether it was helping me with my schoolwork or listening to my continuing complaints about the work H.B. insisted I do.

It was probably at this point in my life that my mother ruined me as a future husband, too. When I lived in my mother's house, I never had to want for clean underwear. Not once. Whenever I went to my drawer, there was always clean underwear neatly folded inside. All mothers want their children to have clean underwear, of course, lest they be in a horrible wreck and the doctor see they are wearing filthy undergarments. I think my mother could have accepted whatever became of me after a wreck, as long as at least one member of the operating team had remarked about how clean my underwear was when the ambulance arrived with me.

Later, when I moved away from home, it became quite clear to me just how important it is to have someone in charge of your underwear. I often would be forced to run through my underwear three and four times before I could no longer stand it and was left with no alternative except to wash my drawers myself. Later, when I married, I found a wife not nearly as concerned about my underwear as my mother had been.

It was the same with food. At an early age, I developed a rather sensitive taste to food. I did not like, for instance, orange juice that came in a can. I preferred the fresh-squeezed variety of orange juice.

My mother would awaken early in the morning and take oranges out of a sack, cut them in half, and then, with her own hands, push them down on one of those old-fashioned juicers. She would then strain the juice in order to get all the seeds out, because I didn't like seeds in my orange juice.

It was the same with French fries. I did not like frozen French fries. They were an affront to my palate. My mother knew this, so she would take out potatoes and cut them just like I liked them—long and thin—and she would fry them in a pan, the grease popping out on her arms and hands the entire time. She also would fry them just like I liked them—crispy on the outside, soggy and greasy on the inside.

If I happened, during my meal, to run across a French fry not to my liking, I would simply say, "Mother, this French fry is not crisp on the outside and soggy and greasy in the middle," and she would remove that French fry from my plate and prepare me one more suitable to take its place.

She always made certain I got the best piece of white meat at Sunday dinner. She bought me a new bicycle when my best friend Danny got one. She bought me an air rifle and didn't take it back when I shot a hole in the window of her bedroom. I was trying to hit a jaybird. The sucker flew away just as I fired.

She allowed me to grow a ducktail haircut when all my

friends started growing them. She bought me new tennis shoes and an expensive new fielder's mitt. She scratched my back when it itched. She cut the fingernails on my right hand. (I mentioned I had bricks for hands; I could never operate a pair of nail clippers with my left hand.) She held my hand when I went to the dentist. She helped me dig the hole in which I buried my dog after he was run over by a car. She didn't put starch in my shirts because I didn't like starch in my shirts. She didn't make me wear shoes until the first frost had fallen. One of the Garfield brothers finally did thrash me on my way home from school one afternoon; she didn't say anything to the boy afterwards, because she knew that would put me in line for another thrashing. She didn't make me go to Wednesday night prayer meeting. She cooked pancakes whenever I asked for them. She gave me money for camp, came to visit me on Parents Day, looked at the merit badges I had earned, and slipped me another couple of dollars for the soft drink machine as she left. She ironed my blue jeans. And the first time my heart was broken, she was there to make it all better.

V

Do Training Bras Have Wheels? Or, I Lost My Love to a '48 Ford

I FIRST NOTICED THERE was something special about girls when they put up the new calendar at Bohannon's Service Station in Moreland. Bohannon's was a gathering place for the town's menfolk, who came to watch Bogator Green, the world-famous auto mechanic, install new manifolds and to talk about women.

I had listened intently to their jokes and comments, but was not yet well-versed enough in such areas of knowledge to understand their meaning.

The standard greeting between the older boys and the men always seemed to be the question, "Gettin' any?"

I thought they were talking about fishing, but I did begin to get somewhat suspicious when Shorty Knowles answered one day by saying, "Not much. My wife's done cut me down to twice a week."

"That's pretty bad, Shorty," somebody spoke up.

"I guess I ought to count my blessings," he replied. "She's done cut two other fellers clean out."

I also noticed that whenever Ronnie Bodenhammer came by the station, the men would circle around him and he would hold their attention for some time with what I learned later were tales of countywide romantic involvements. Ronnie also had a habit of scratching his privates during these sessions, and one of my older friends later explained that was an indication he was "gettin' a lot." That is when I threw my fishing theory completely out the window.

But I digress. The new calendar, which was sent to Bohannon's each year by a parts company, always attracted a lot of attention. It was sort of like the opening of a new showing at an art gallery.

The first year I remember taking more than a casual glance at the picture that accompanied the calendar was when I was seven. The woman pictured on the calendar was without benefit of any sort of clothing. She was bent over and smiling as she winked at the camera. By today's bare-it-all standards, there was not really that much to see; but in 1953, the photo on the calendar drew gawkers from as far away as Grantville to the south and Arnco-Sargent to the north, and somebody said a man came all the way from Griffin to see it.

I quietly and patiently waited until there was no one tall standing in front of me so I could see the picture. I looked at it for a time, and I did feel some strange sensation befalling me. It was as if I were feeling some rare excitement but could not identify the source of it.

I was cast out of my whimsy, however, when one of the men noticed me staring at the picture.

"Whatchu lookin' at, son?" he asked.

The other men around him started laughing, and I was thoroughly embarrassed and ran all the way home. I knew, however, I had taken perhaps my first nibble off some wildly delicious fruit, and I was determined to know more.

You can't keep a secret from a good man very long. One of my friends was rambling around in his house one day and found what he thought was a balloon, after he cracked open a small packet that resembled a large coin. He blew up the balloon, tied a knot in one end, and was bouncing it around the house, when his father came home and spent two hours trying to untie the knot in the end of the balloon.

Realizing his son might make the same error at some time in the future, he sat him down, explained the basics of the reproductive process to him, and implored him to keep his hands off any future balloons he might find lying around the house.

My friend couldn't wait to spill the beans to the rest of us, and one thing led to another, and pretty soon we had the entire thing down pat. What gaps were left in the story were easily filled by older friends and relatives, including my older female cousin, who had heard of a girl in Newnan who actually did it with any boy who wanted to. She had only a first name, but the girl became a sort of legend to me and my friends. I think had we actually ever seen her, we would have all fainted.

We got even more graphic information the day Pug Boatright brought to school the deck of cards his brother had brought home from the Navy. This was no ordinary deck of cards. Each carried a black-and-white photograph of grown people actually doing it right there before your very eyes. Each participant had a black bar across his or her face in order to remain anonymous. One of the men looked a little like Ronnie Bodenhammer, but we couldn't be sure.

Pug made a virtual killing renting out the cards by the hour and the day, and he might have retired a wealthy man by the time he reached the fourth grade, had his brother not called the cards back in when his Navy leave expired.

With a full brace of knowledge about what was what, the next question that came to our minds was, did the girls in our class actually understand all this, too? If they knew it, we all secretly hoped, then maybe there might be that one minuscule chance in a million that they might even do it.

These were simpler times. Even married couples on television slept in separate beds. One of my friends reported one day that he had it on good authority that a particular girl in our class did, indeed, have a full working knowledge of this magnificent thing. But when we questioned her, she hadn't even heard that if you scratched a girl in her palm with your finger and she scratched you back, it meant that she was ready to do it. So we dismissed her as a charlatan and were all quite disappointed at this turn of events.

The key breakthrough came when rumors abounded that one of the fifth-grade boys, who lived in a sharecropper's shack, had to sleep with his seventh-grade sister because of a shortage of beds, and that they had actually, positively, without question, done it. She had told him that all the girls knew everything there was to know, but weren't going to talk about it until they were married.

The utter thrill of it all! Somebody we actually knew, somebody we saw on the playground, had actually done it. And on top of that, every girl in our class was totally aware of every, single, solitary detail, and one day we might even force one to admit it! This possibility kept us all fraught with enthusiasm and expectation. One afternoon at a church picnic at Raymond Lake, a group of us wandered away—three boys and three girls—and, off behind a cluster of pine trees, we bluntly asked the girls if they knew about . . . well, doing it.

"My mother told me three years ago," said one of the girls, with a touch of arrogance in her voice.

"My sister showed me some pictures from her biology book in high school," added another. "The sperm goes into the . . . ."

We asked her to spare us any more of the details, we by-god knew exactly where the sperm went, and we didn't need some girl to tell us.

The other girl said her older sister went out with Ronnie Bodenhammer recently, and that he tried to get her to lie down in the back seat of his car.

Ol' Ronnie Bodenhammer! What a man was he! No

wonder he scratched his privates so much, the man was a h-o-u-n-d, hound!

We wanted more details. Did her sister get into the back of ol' Ronnie's car and lie down?

"No," said the girl. "He kept scratching his wing-wong, and she was afraid she might catch the clap."

The clap? What was this clap?

"Oh, you know, silly," the girl explained. "Venereal disease. VD. Syphilis and gonorrhea, sexually transmitted diseases that make you swell up and go blind."

Swell up and go blind?

"You little boys don't know a thing," said the girl who knew so much about where the sperm went. "Come back to see us when you grow up."

The girls went back to the church picnic; we sat quietly in the woods for a long time, and then made a pact not to mention any of this to anybody.

*   *   *

The first time I officially fell in love was in the seventh grade. I was twelve. What attracted me to her was the fact that a friend of mine said he saw the girl—her name was Shirley Ann—shopping for a training bra in a Newnan department store with her mother. It stood to reason that if she needed a training bra, there must, in fact, be something that needed training.

I'm not certain when girls actually began developing breasts, but it seemed to me that some of the girls in my class sprouted theirs overnight. One day they were as flat as Pug Boatright's nose, and the next day their sweaters had come alive right before my eyes.

That didn't happen to all the girls, however. Laura Gaines comes to mind as a perfect example of the exception to the rule.

Laura's lack of breast development was a source of great anguish and embarrassment to her, quite obviously. When she was thirteen and all her girlfriends were blossoming into womanhood, she still had the body of an undernourished nine-year-old boy; she could still go shirtless to the swimming pool, six miles down the road in Grantville, and remain virtually unnoticed.

The pressure on her to grow breasts was further increased by the fact that she was subject to much ridicule. It was a rather cruel yet common practice for the boys to go up to Laura and say, "Hey Laura, I'm going to tell you a joke that will make you laugh your boobs off. . . . Oh, I see you've already heard it."

Laura tried everything to grow breasts. There was one commonly-held belief that if a girl slept on her stomach, her breasts would be slow to develop. Laura slept on her back for years, and even refused to lie face down when we had practice tornado drills in our school. That didn't help, however.

She also ordered a jar of breast-development cream she had read about in a movie magazine, but all that did was cost her $4.95 for what was basically a jar of teat balm, normally used to relieve the pain of over-milked cows.

She eventually resorted to prayer, but apparently the Lord misunderstood her, because instead of her breasts growing larger, her feet suddenly increased in size to the point that she resembled a very tall, flat-chested duck.

However, it is important to note here that one can never predict what might eventually happen when it comes to girls' breasts. When Laura was seventeen, a marvelous thing happened. Her breasts suddenly grew to fit her feet. The eruption caused a great deal of comment about and interest in the previously lonely and lamentable Laura. It caused every flat-chested girl in the county to develop a renewed interest in the power of prayer.

As I grew older, I would retain my own interest in girls' breasts, and I would learn that no matter what size breasts some girls had, they would resort to almost any devious method to make boys think they were actually larger.

Among the items girls were known to push down into their brassieres to make their breasts appear larger were tissue paper, socks, aluminum foil, cotton, biscuit dough, wads of newspaper, stuffed quilt patches, stuffed animals, sewing cushions, heads of cabbage, and the standard foam rubber.

I once met a girl at the beach when I was in high school and asked her to go in for a swim with me. Everything was fine until we stepped off a sandbar together. The water came all the way up to my neck. She sunk only to the top of her bathing suit, and was suddenly a good two heads taller than me. It was some time before I figured out that the protrusion in her bathing suit was mostly padding; she could have floated halfway across the Atlantic.

I would also learn later that whoever was responsible for inventing the chastity belt likely had a hand in creating the brassiere, as well. In broad daylight, it is basically impossible to unsnap a brassiere, regardless of whether the snap is in the front or the back. In the dark, when most attempts are made to unsnap brassieres by those not actually wearing them at the time, one needs the hands of a surgeon and a degree in engineering from M.I.T.

The first time a girl ever agreed to allow me to unsnap her bra, I spent fifteen minutes fumbling with the snap and never did get it off. Worse, in my effort to contort my body into a position to get a better grip, I pulled a muscle in my side and got a crick in my neck.

The first time I ever actually saw a pair of breasts live was at the county fair, which featured Boom-Boom LaTouche and her famous "Airplane Dance." The barker outside the tent explained in a very loud voice that Miss LaTouche would first engage in a "take-off," and "then you oughta see her tailspin, boys!"

Two friends and I paid a quarter each to get inside; we were quite surprised they would allow boys our age to watch such a spectacle. We were filled with anticipation for what we were about to see.

Boom-Boom, a rather large woman with a number of bovine-like features, came out in a costume that fit her like skin on a sausage, popped out of it with a quick wiggle and a shake, and what unfolded there in front of my very eyes were two huge mounds that she could make go up and down and around and around. That was enough to marvel at as it was, but then she showed even more amazing control of her endowments by making them circle around from her belly button to just under her chin in opposite directions. My friends and I joined the rest of the assemblage in giving Boom-Boom a much-deserved standing ovation.

Again, I digress, however. After hearing the report of Shirley Ann's shopping for a training bra, I anxiously awaited the next day of school to see if, and how, her appearance had changed. I broke into an immediate cold sweat, and my heart began to pound when she walked into the classroom wearing a sweater that featured two small, yet distinct, pointed growths that certainly had not been there the last time she had worn that, or any other, sweater.

I never actually got to touch Shirley Ann's trainees with my hands, but the first time I closed my eyes and drew her close to me for a slow dance, I did feel something pushing into my chest, and I was filled with ecstasy. What I felt, however, turned out to be her nose. Shirley Ann was quite short, even for a seventh grader.

Our love affair grew steadily. I tried to make her aware of my affection for her in a myriad of ways, not the least of which was changing my dog's name from "Duke"—in honor of my favorite baseball player, Duke Snider of the Dodgers—to "Shirley Ann."

My girlfriend was quite flattered by this, but my dog growled at me every time I called him after that, as if to say, "Don't call me Shirley Ann, or I'll bite off your toes."

I also bought her popsicles after school, or, because I was not exactly well-off financially at the time, I would buy one popsicle, break it apart, and give her one stick and keep the other. After licking away at a stick of popsicle,

Shirley Ann was a vision of loveliness with grape all over her gums and tongue.

As much as I dearly loved her, and as much as she seemed to enjoy my companionship, I could sense our days were numbered when we entered the eighth grade and we both turned thirteen.

When girls turn thirteen, they are suddenly open game for boys in high school. When boys turn thirteen, it means absolutely nothing, except they're too old for Little League and still three years away from obtaining their driver's license.

As long as a girl isn't thirteen yet, it is possible to hold her attention with walks back and forth to school, a little smoochie-woochie on the way home from MYF, an occasional movie where your mother drops you off and then picks you up again, and popsicle-sharing and dog-renaming in her honor.

Afterwards, however, girls turn their attention away from such timid activities, and begin to think about all the possibilities a boy old enough to drive an automobile could provide them.

From thirteen until sixteen is probably the toughest period of a male's life. He is certainly old enough to want to graduate from what few romantic opportunities the preteen years provide, but he is not yet old enough to do anything about it. It isn't really true that girls mature faster than boys, it's just that they are able to discover the back seat of a 1957 Chevrolet long before boys their same age have the same opportunity.

Willard Haines, who had just turned sixteen and who had been given not a 1957 Chevrolet but a 1948 Ford for his birthday, began to show an increasing amount of interest in Shirley Ann at Sunday School.

Shirley Ann's sweaters were growing more and more interesting with every day that passed, and the pangs of jealousy I had felt when my mother first began dating my stepfather came rushing back with a fierce intensity.

Willard did what every other sixteen-year-old with his first car was obliged to do. He put taps on the bottom of his shoes, started smoking Luckies and rolled them up in the left sleeve of his T-shirt, hung a pair of foam rubber dice on the rear-view mirror of his car, and installed loud mufflers that sounded like the start of the Darlington 500 every time he cranked his engine. He also developed the ability every new male driver must have in order to compete with his peers—the talent to peel a wheel whenever more than two were gathered to watch him drive away. How could half of a stupid grape popsicle compete with that?

I lost my darling Shirley Ann in the blink of an eye, the beat of a heart, the sudden lurch of a '48 Ford, and the screech of two soon-to-be-worn Armstrong tires.

Many were the nights I would lie in my bed and hear Willard Haines' car roaring down the blacktop road near my house, knowing full well that with the changing of every gear and with the subsequent squalling of his tires, my first love was getting farther and farther away. Willard Haines had my girlfriend, and all I had was a dog who hated me for making him the laughingstock of the canine community.

Well, that's not all I had. I had my mother, of course, and I went to her with my fractured heart.

"Have you tried talking to Shirley Ann and telling her how much you care for her?" my mother asked me, tenderly.

"I even offered to let her have the entire popsicle next time," I said.

"I know how it hurts, son," my mother continued, "but just remember that no matter what happens to you or how much you are hurt, your mother will always love you."

For the first time in my life, I realized there was an occasion now, and there would be occasions in the future, when that wouldn't be enough.

VI

Happiness Is a Red-Headed Cheerleader

BUN WORD DIED in the spring of my first year in high school. He was seventy-three, yet he was still working his fields just as hard as before. Even after my mother and stepfather and I moved into our new house, I spent many evenings with him. My grandparents had a television by then, and he and I watched it together.

He enjoyed baseball games, wrestling matches, westerns, and Billy Graham specials. He hated "The Ed Sullivan Show," because most weeks about all Ed had to offer was a magician or two, some trained seals, and an opera singer.

We were watching the program one Sunday evening anyway, and Ed Sullivan introduced Anna Maria Alberghetti, who shook the windows with her voice. Daddy Bun watched and listened for a few moments and then replied,

"If that woman can sing, my ass is a typewriter." As he walked out of the room, he said to me, "Call me when the seals come out."

The old mule had died by then, and Daddy Bun was following his little Briggs and Stratton garden tractor up a row one April afternoon when he felt the first pains in his chest. He was never one to complain, but the pains became so intense that he struggled back to his house and sat down in a chair, hoping the crushing feeling would go away. My grandmother knew there was something wrong by the fact that he had come inside, apparently to rest. Nothing could bring him in from the fields, short of gully-washing rain.

"Are you all right, Daddy?" she asked him.

He did not reply, however. He hurt too much to speak.

My grandmother rushed to our house, and my mother and I went to him and somehow managed to get him inside our car. We drove him to the only hospital in the county, six miles away in Newnan. He revived a bit on the way, and by the time he was rolled into the emergency room, he had already started to apologize to everyone for causing a disturbance.

A day later, he had improved to the point he was begging to go home from the hospital and get back to his fields. The doctors dismissed him the day after he had been admitted. They did advise him, however, to slow down a bit, but he didn't listen. His family had been advising him to ease off on his work for years, but without his garden and his tractor, he likely wouldn't have lived as long as he did.

Four days after he came home from the hospital, I had

supper with my grandparents. Mama Willie made her square-ended cornbread and fried a hen. Daddy Bun seemed in uncommonly good spirits that night. After eating, we played a couple of hands of Rook, and then I left to attend revival services at the Baptist church a few yards from my grandparents' house.

The visiting preacher was just about to call for the invitational hymn, "Just As I Am," when one of my cousins came into the church and whispered something to my mother, who was sitting next to me.

She jumped out of her seat and ran toward the door. I suppose I knew what was happening, even without having been told, but I didn't want to believe it.

When I reached my grandparents' house, H.B. was bent over Daddy Bun, who was lying in his bed. My mother and my Aunt Jessie were crying, and Mama Willie's face was frozen with fear.

Daddy Bun's eyes were closed, and his face was turning blue. H.B., a large man with powerful arms, was pushing on his chest, attempting to start his heart beating. The ambulance arrived and they put Daddy Bun on the stretcher. I held the front door open as they rolled him down the steps. My grandfather's mouth was open and there was no sign of life to him.

Somebody said later that he probably died in his bed. Mama Willie said she thought he did, too, and she would give this account of the final moments she shared with her husband of more than fifty years:

"I had just turned off the light," she began, "and Daddy was on his side of the bed, and I was on mine. All of a sudden, he rolled over and put his arm around me, and he kissed me and he tried to say something, but I felt him go limp. And when I tried to get him to answer me, he didn't say anything."

One last kiss and then he died. Even at fourteen, I was charmed and warmed by that, and there was something else that pleased me, too. I remember that my grandmother never went to bed with snuff in her mouth.

The funeral took all day. First, we drove back to his home church, Pleasant Grove Baptist in Heard County, and three preachers I had never seen before took turns at the pulpit. It was just the kind of service my grandfather would have wanted.

None of the three preachers had any prepared notes, I was positive, because nobody could have read that fast. They would start out slowly, but by the time each had reached the climax of his message, his coat would be off, his tie would be undone, his shirt would be wringing wet with perspiration, and he would be gasping for breath every five or six sentences that would come rushing out of his mouth in powerful gusts. It was impossible to keep up with what the preachers were trying to say, but I was able to pick up a "Pah-raise his name!" here and a "Have you been washed in the buh-lud?" there, and so I at least knew the general subject matter.

There were a couple of things I would have changed about my grandfather's funeral, however. It was the custom then to bring a body back home after the undertaker had completed his work, and friends and family would then gather, and one by one they would stand over the casket and peer in at the departed. The closest family members usually broke down when they looked at the body of their loved one, but friends usually didn't cry. they simply stared awhile and then remarked, "Lord, Lord, he looks like he could just sit up and talk, don't he?"

Actually, my grandfather didn't look like he could just sit up and talk at all, and even if he had, his first words likely would have been an apology for the way he was dressed. They put him in a banker's suit and put a white shirt and a tie on him, and they took off his glasses. And if I hadn't been with him practically every day of my life since I was seven, I might not have recognized him.

They should have dressed him in one of his old shirts and in his work pants, and they shouldn't have put all that powdery gook on his face. And had it been left up to me, I would have put the *Market Bulletin* in the casket with him, so that when he got to heaven, he could have looked in the classifieds at what they were getting for mules around the state, one of his favorite pastimes.

After the services in Heard County, we brought him all the way back to Moreland to bury him in the family plot. Unfortunately, there had been no more room available in the Baptist cemetery near his house when Daddy Bun and Mama Willie decided it was time to plan for where they would go to rest. So they had reluctantly bought in the Methodist cemetery a mile or so away from their home.

There was one other thing I would have changed. It was, indeed, fitting that they had a girl from the community sing "What a Friend We Have in Jesus" when we got to his graveside, but I would have asked her to hum the last two verses.

Mama Willie refused to move out of their little house after Daddy Bun died. I didn't blame her very much, and I even agreed to spend the night with her in my old bedroom. She wasn't in the best of health, either, and the family was afraid to leave her alone nights.

My grandmother changed a lot after Daddy Bun died. She wasn't nearly as spirited. Her memory began to go. I could hear her talking to "Daddy" in her sleep, and sometimes, when I sat with her at night, her conversation would wander, and she would discuss occurrences of long ago as if I were Daddy Bun. I never tried to correct her, and I actually enjoyed sharing with her some of the things she had shared with him. I also made certain that at least once a week, when I came down to her house to spend the night, I brought a little can of Brutton's with me.

"You always were a sweet boy," she would say to me. I sort of wished she would send me for one more switch, just for old times' sake.

*   *   *

After children from the little community of Moreland finished the eighth grade, they were then picked up in county buses in front of the old schoolhouse each morning and transported to Newnan High School, a huge educational plant that was quite unsettling to those of us from the hinterlands.

We also were confronted with some difficulty in being totally accepted by our classmates who had grown up in Newnan, one of the wealthiest towns per capita in the country. None of the Moreland boys had the word that white socks were out, for instance, and we first laughed at the colorful footwear the Newnan boys sported before we found out they were the very latest style at a dollar-fifty a pair.

We also learned that the correct shoe to wear was made by Bass and was called a "Wee-Jun," that Madras shirts were a must and they should have a button in the back of the collar, that pants needed to be pegged at the cuff so that the colored socks would show, and that if you didn't have a beige London Fog raincoat to wear, you were a total country hick whose social opportunities were limited to showing a hog or a cow at the Future Farmers of America-sponsored agriculture show at the annual county fair.

I had no intentions of being ostracized thusly, so I went to my mother after my third day of high school and asked her for money to purchase myself a new wardrobe. When she heard that colored socks cost a dollar-fifty a pair, and that I had to have shirts that were imported from India, along with other expensive accessories, she nearly fainted. She was still bringing home the meager salary of a county elementary schoolteacher, and my stepfather had fallen on hard times trying to sell a-dollar-and-a-deed-is-all-you-need shell homes.

She wouldn't go more than two pairs of socks, one Madras shirt, and a couple of pairs of new pants, but she did allow me at least that. I helped my Uncle Hugh Dorsey pull his corn one entire weekend for half what the Wee-Juns cost, and I got the rest by selling "Pig" Landers my lunchroom dessert every day for a month. Pig had an appetite that was legend. One day when we were still in grammar school in Moreland, some of the men who used to play checkers in front of Cureton and Cole's store asked

Pig if he thought he could eat a particularly large watermelon that was for sale in the store.

"We'll buy it if you can eat it," they said to Pig, who surprised us by asking if he could go home first. He returned a few minutes later and said he thought he could, indeed, eat a watermelon that size, and he proceeded to do just that, gnawing well into the rind before he was finished.

"That's some kinda eatin', boy," said one of the men, "but why'd you have to go home first?"

"We had one in the icebox about the same size," said Pig. "I went home and ate that one just to make sure I could eat this one."

Thanks to the generosity of my mother, my corn-pulling efforts, and Pig Landers' appetite, I managed to dress myself in a fashion consistent with that of my more affluent classmates, and afterwards I turned my attention to one of my new school's most exciting benefits.

My eighth grade class in Moreland had totalled less than thirty, and only about half of those were girls, and five or six of them you wouldn't take to a rat-killing. But high school! There were girls everywhere, and more bosoms than I had ever seen under one roof.

(Be ever mindful, however, that I had yet to see but one pair of unclothed breasts, those of the talented Boom-Boom LaTouche. Another chance had gone by the boards later when a group of my friends and I learned through the grapevine that Sherleen Gimple—whose daddy, Farnon, ran a brisk chenille bedspread and memorial marker business out front of his house—always took a tub bath about eight o'clock in the evening, and that if you were quiet about it, it was very possible to climb up in a tree outside the Gimples' bathroom window and get the show of your life. Trembling with the same anticipation that had been ours when we saw Boom-Boom at the fair—and feeling smug in the fact there would be no admission charge—we sneaked up the tree shortly before eight one evening and waited for Sherleen, who had a set known for miles around, to take her bath.

When the light went on, we could barely keep from welcoming Sherleen with a rousing cheer, but imagine our disappointment when the figure we saw through the window was fat old Farnon Gimple taking off his overalls. The one night we chose to try to get a glimpse of Sherleen, her daddy decided to take his weekly bath.)

Despite the fact the female population at Newnan High was larger than what I was used to by a hundredfold, I was still being hampered in replacing the long-gone Shirley Ann by two factors:

One, I had just turned fourteen and was still two long, agonizing years away from having my driver's license. Whereas Willard Haines and only a few other older boys in Moreland had cars, high school was filled with licensees from the eleventh and twelfth grades, and they were constantly shopping in the lower grades for dates, because girls their age were dating college boys by that time. Obtaining female companionship in the formative years is an eat-the-next-fish-smaller-than-you sort of proposition.

Two, and this is something I hadn't counted on, there was a sort of loose, unwritten rule that implored county riffraff to keep away from the well-coiffed, well-dressed young ladies of the city establishment. That problem could be overcome, I noticed, if one happened to be an athlete or was willing to settle for one of the uglier Newnan girls, who were just as desperate for attention as the county fellows.

I decided to try the athletic route. Because I had taken my physical appearance from my mother's side of the family—I was quite thin—I decided not to risk my life playing football, as much as I figured that was the sport with the most potential for latching on to a Newnan girl. Instead, I went out for the junior varsity basketball team. I made the squad and became an immediate starter.

I thought perhaps my first move would be on a member of the girls' junior varsity team; but it was at that point I learned something else about females of that era—if they played basketball, it meant they hadn't made it as a cheerleader and didn't mind working up a sweat in public, both of which made me suspect of their potential, as far as future romantic possibilities were concerned.

I also stayed as far away as possible from the girls' basketball team in high school, because good ol' Alice McTavish from Virginia Reel days was a member, and she had grown even bigger and stronger. I remained constantly afraid that she would rekindle her affection for me, and I didn't think my frail physique could take it, especially now that the Twist was the popular dance of the time. She might have caught me broadside with one of her hips, and I could see myself rolling across the dance floor as Chubby Checker sang away.

The way they played girls' basketball in those days was three girls, the forwards, shot at the basket while three others, the guards, played defense on the other end. It didn't really matter how they played when Alice McTavish was in the game, however.

One of the problems most women have in sports is their basic inability to jump very high. There wasn't a girl in the state who could get above Alice McTavish's out-reached, blacksmith-like arms. The Newnan offense was simply for Alice to stand under the basket. When the ball was passed to her, she turned and shot it at the hoop.

It would seem that Newnan would have been a power-house in girls' basketball, with Godzilla underneath the basket, but Alice was as clumsy and as uncoordinated as she was ugly and large. Often she would shoot the ball over and over again, getting her own rebound each time, only to have time to run out in the quarter before she could get the ball into the basket. Newnan lost a great many 8-6 games in girls' basketball during the McTavish era.

Alice was rarely called on to dribble. However, in a close game one night, she received a pass from the guards over the center line, and turned only to find herself still several feet out of what may be loosely referred to as her shooting range.

It never occurred to her to pass the ball to one of her teammates, and the sight of Alice trying to dribble the ball toward the basket had everyone in the gym howling with laughter. After a couple of bounces, the ball went sailing off one of Alice's size-fourteen high-tops and out of bounds. Alice put her hands on her hips and, in a voice that could best be described as a bellow, uttered an unprintable oath loud enough for the entire audience and the people in line at the concession stand to hear it.

The referee standing closest to her had no choice but to

attempt to eject her from the game. Alice refused to sit down, however, and when the official insisted, she let him have one in the belly. Alice continued to play the remainder of the game. They called one of the shop teachers to come out of the stands to take the injured referee's place, while he was trying to catch his breath

Having thus decided to avoid girl basketball players, I turned my attention to the cheerleaders. Making cheerleader at Newnan High School was a great and highly sought-after honor. The students elected the cheerleading team after a series of tryouts, in which each entrant was asked to perform a series of cheers and acrobatics in front of the entire student body. Girls were supposed to be chosen on the basis of originality of cheer, tumbling ability, range of voice, and whether or not they would be outstanding representatives of their school, community, and parents during interscholastic events. I always voted on the basis of which girl showed the most of her underpants when she whirled around in her cheerleading skirt.

The first cheerleader to catch my eye during my freshman year of high school was a dazzling fourteen-year-old redhead from a well-to-do Newnan family. She whirled with the best of them, and she did seem to show some spark of interest when I hit her with my classic opening line, "Do you think professional wrestling is fake?"

As a matter of fact, I fell quite hard and fast for this young beauty, and I thought I had scored further points with her when I allowed her to look on my paper during an ancient history exam, which tested our knowledge of the Punic Wars. She had no idea Rome and Carthage were even mad at each other, much less that they had actually squared off on the fields of combat.

I was soon to learn, however, that this new object of my affection didn't care if I was a brilliant conversationalist and more than willing to share my knowledge of ancient history with her. She already had a boyfriend, and he was an eleventh grader, with a car, who played football. I thought of trying the old popsicle trick on her, and my dog wouldn't have anything to do with me as it was, so what difference would one more name change make?

However, I finally accepted the fact these tactics were no longer workable on any girl over twelve. I simply had no way to fight back against the overwhelming odds that faced me. I looked ahead, and all I could see were two more years of being just another skinny basketball player from the sticks, whose mother still had to drive him around. I thought of petitioning the state legislature to lower the driving age in order to save me from this companionless state, but in my most desperate hour, I got lucky. It all started with a hayride.

VII

Billy Graham
Looks a Lot
Like God

PRACTICALLY EVERY ASPECT of life in Moreland revolved around the town's two churches. I had been born into a Methodist family, and when my mother and I moved back to Moreland, we joined the white-frame Moreland Methodist Church that sat in a shady grove on the town square, or what was left of it after the boll weevil and the Depression had closed down the bank and the cotton gin.

Moreland Baptist sat just across Highway 27 in back of the Methodist church. The town was divided fairly evenly between sprinklers and submergers. The Baptists may have had a slight edge membership-wise, but the Methodists tended to offer a better spread at the frequent dinners-on-the-grounds, that were traditionally held whenever a month happened to offer a fifth Sunday. Baptists normally conducted a more austere lifestyle than did the Moreland Methodists—they put off buying their first television sets and installing indoor plumbing a lot longer, for instance—and Baptist chicken never seemed quite as plump and tender to me as Methodist chicken.

The Methodists had another advantage when it came to food, because among their members were Opal Evans and Maxine Estes, both of whom were to fried chicken what Chef Boy-Ar-Dee is to canned spaghetti. Each had her own distinctive style. Opal went for a thin, light crust, especially attractive to those members of the congregation who wore dentures, while Maxine's crust was much crispier. I normally preferred Opal's drumsticks and Maxine's pulley-bones.

Besides the chicken, there was also country ham and pork chops, and marvelous things had been done to sweet potatoes. And there were fresh garden vegetables, and homemade biscuits, and cornbread, and home-baked pies and cakes, and to wash all this down, there was always a large tub filled with tea that swirled around a piece of block ice. One more advantage to the Methodist feeds was that the pre-meal blessing was a lot shorter than the one normally offered before the Baptists took plates in hand and had at it.

Normally, the minister at the Methodist church would call for everyone's attention and then call on Wes Tidwell to give thanks. Wes, fortunately for all gathered with plates-in-hand, was a man of few words. A simple "Make us thankful, Lord, for these and all our many blessings. Amen," was about all Wes figured the Lord wanted to hear, if he was as hungry as the rest of us. Down at the

Baptist church, however, if the minister happened to call on one of the more longwinded of his deacons, the ants would have already covered the chocolate cake and the block of ice would have melted half away by the time he was finished asking for remembrance of all the sick and shut-in, praying for rain and guidance for our state and local leaders, and asking a blessing on each individual dish, even the boiled okra somebody always brought, despite the fact that nobody ever ate any of it, not even the ants.

There also tended to be a bit more disharmony at the Baptist church. The congregation split on the matter of building a baptismal pool behind the pulpit, for instance. Previously, all baptisms had taken place in a church-owned pond located in a wooded area a half-mile from the church. Because of the walk involved, attendance at baptizings was not good, and because the water in the pond was often stagnant and covered with scum and water bugs, the number of new dunkees was also dwindling.

Many in the congregation felt an inside pool was the modern, clean, and efficient way to go, while the more fundamentalist thinkers in the church pointed out that nowhere in the Bible was there any mention of anybody ever being baptized in what would amount to a galvanized hog trough. After weeks of heated debate, the issue was put to a vote. The new, inside baptismal pool won out by a scant three votes, and a motion was also carried on the coattails of that vote to drain the Baptist pond.

I had never seen a pond drained before, and when they broke the dam and allowed the water to pour into the surrounding woods, I was amazed at what remained on the muddy bottom. Besides enough catfish to feed the entire county for a month and turtles the size of grown hogs, there were also several cases of empty liquor and beer bottles, the rusted hull of what at one time had been a Packard, a mattress, several articles of clothing, and what appeared to be a truck radiator with a number of circular tubes running out of it. Many of those who had voted against draining the pond were not present for the dam breaking, incidentally.

A movement to install a new chandelier in the sanctuary also brought up some discord. A number of the members felt an expenditure for such an item was out of the question, while others thought a chandelier would bring dignity to the church. One member stood up and said he thought a piano was the only musical instrument the church needed, and what the money should be spent for was some new lights instead of for a chandelier. The chandelier was eventually voted down in favor of chimes that would be played each Sunday morning and evening, and on Wednesday nights before prayer meetings. Later, that caused trouble, too, however, when one of the members, who raised turkeys, complained that the chimes made his birds nervous. The man almost convinced the church to take out the chimes, when those who lived near his farm realized what sort of aroma three thousand nervous turkeys might possibly emit. A compromise motion was passed, calling for the church to give the chimes and the turkeys a rest on Wednesday prayer meeting nights.

Although I remained steadfast in my Methodist leanings, I spent a great deal of time at the Baptist church, too. I always made it to their summer revivals, and often I would drop in at their Baptist Training Union (BTU) meetings on the way home from Methodist Youth Fellowship (MYF), in case I still had a taste for refreshments. I also attended Vacation Bible School at both churches, thereby providing myself with not one, but two weeks of free soft drinks and cookies, as well as further opportunities to socialize with my friends.

My best friend, Danny Thompson, was a Baptist, as a matter of fact, and we were inseparable in those days. Danny could run much faster than I could, but I knew the capitals of every state in the union, and so after he would thrash me in an afternoon of footracing, we would sit down under a large tree in his yard, and I would amaze him with my ability to give a capital for every state he could name, including Montpelier for Vermont and Pierre for South Dakota.

Danny and I were sitting next to each other at Baptist Bible School the first time I ever saw Paula. It was the summer between our fifth and sixth grade years. We were still only barely tolerant of girls in those days, and when the tall, gangly child walked into our Bible School class, Danny asked me, "Who is that?"

"Never seen her before in my life," I replied.

"I wonder if she's going to be in our class?" Danny continued.

"I hope not," I answered him. "She looks like she's been sick a lot to me."

The truth of the matter was that she—Paula—was simply in that growth stage in which little girls suddenly sprout long arms and legs, and take a shape roughly akin to those tall Africans you occasionally see on television, who can high jump over a thatch hut by getting a running start and then leaping off huge ant mounds.

When she walked, she moved with a sort of forward tilt, as if she were fighting a strong headwind. She also had a long nose and a weird sort of hairstyle that likely had come from a Toni home permanent box.

She did, in fact, enter the sixth grade with us, and that is when I noticed a couple of other things about her that disturbed me. One, she talked entirely too much, and two, she was left-handed, and when she wrote, she hooked her hand around and sort of drug the pencil backwards.

The first words I ever said to her were, "Where did you learn to write like that?"

"What's wrong with the way I write?" was her response.

I happened to be right at the top of my class in penmanship and considered myself quite the expert on the subject.

"You slant your letters the wrong way," I explained. "Plus, the way you hook your hand around the top of each line and the way you hold your pencil looks stupid."

"Well," she countered, "you have freckles all over your face and your front teeth overlap, and I'll write any way I please."

I've always had a way with women.

That was the last time we spoke until the summer before we started high school. One day I saw Paula, and she was still jumping over thatch huts with those long legs of hers; the next day, each part of her was suddenly in rather pleasing proportion with the other parts, and the way she looked when walking away from me in a pair of tight-fitting shorts made me forget about the strange way she held a pencil. Her nose didn't seem nearly as long as it had before, either; her hair was longer and, for the first time, I noticed she had perfect, white teeth that didn't overlap in the front like mine did. If a thirteen-year-old can look sultry, she most certainly did.

As I began to realize that my hopes of finding romantic involvement with one of the girls from Newnan were fading, I began to give serious consideration to this Paula, who had walked into my life at Bible School three years earlier. I still had the problem of not being old enough to drive, however, and there was also the fact that engaging in any activity with me ranked next-to-last on Paula's list of pleasant occurrences. An outbreak of pimples on her nose ranked dead last, and the two options weren't that far apart, in her mind.

I wish I could say that the funny way I turned my head when I laughed, or my witty-yet-warm personality, or the casual-but-elegant way I carried myself had something to do with winning her over, but it didn't. I owe the whole thing to the Baptist Church, my friend Danny Thompson, and Billy Graham.

First, the church. Several times each year, the Baptist Training Union youth group planned such social outings as watermelon cuttings, swimming parties to Grantville, rat-killings at someone's barn, marshmallow roasts, and hayrides. The younger kids were still very much enthralled with the rat-killings, but the older children had developed a deep sense of appreciation for the hayride, which worked this way, I was soon to discover:

Somebody donated a tractor, which one of the adult chaperones would drive. The tractor would then pull a wagon filled with hay on a long drive out into the woods. The idea was to sit in the hay and sing a few rousing songs, and then maybe roast a wienie or two at mid-ride. Another adult would sit with the kids in the back on the hay wagon, to answer any questions that might come up about the Sermon on the Mount, or how to say "no" to such pleasures of the flesh as drinking, smoking, or fooling around.

However, this was all just theory. What really happened on hayrides is the adult driving the tractor had his back turned to everything anyway, so he couldn't see, or stop, what was going on, and the adult on guard in the wagon was powerless to stop fifteen couples involved in mostly light, with occasional gusts to moderate, petting.

How my friend Danny Thompson got involved in all this is that he had been smitten by my cousin Melba, Uncle Hugh Dorsey's blonde youngest, and, both being members of the BTU, they decided to accompany one another on the upcoming hayride. Since each member could invite another person of their choice, they each had an unused invitation.

I was in the drugstore in Newnan reading magazines when Danny approached me with the idea of attending the hayride. Reading magazines in the drugstore was a Saturday afternoon ritual with me. My mother would drive into town to do her grocery shopping and I would go along, ostensibly to help her with the grocery bags. What I really wanted to do, however, was to get a few free peeks at what, in those pre-*Playboy* days, were termed "men's magazines."

There were *Saga* and *Argosy,* to name a couple, magazines filled with mostly adventure stories about shooting antelope. However, if one were diligent enough in his search, one could also find a picture or two of scantily clad women. The editors of those magazines were smart enough to know they couldn't hold their readership with a dead antelope or two each month, so they would offer a smattering of soft-core stories and photographs, which wouldn't even make Rev. Jerry Falwell blush today, but which were more than enough to arouse my developing prurient interests back then.

I looked forward to these Saturday forays into pornography's early stages, and normally warmed up during the week with a casual glance or two through the women's underwear section of the Sears, Roebuck catalog.

Looking at photographs of fat women in corsets wasn't very titillating, but Sears came through each season with at least a page or two of young models in bras and panties. My grandmother caught me looking at the ladies in their Sears underthings one day, and subsequently hid the catalog and would not give me access to it again until I promised to look at nothing more arousing than garden tractors and shotguns.

Movie ads, especially those featuring Jane Russell, were also worthwhile in my continuing search for the feminine form at least partially unveiled, as were copies of the *National Geographic* that came to the school library each month. I had no interest whatsoever in pictorials featuring kangaroos or the Yangtze River, but I did spend many a library hour poring over the pages in search of anything that had to do with equatorial societies, where topless maidens made pottery. No subscriber to the *National*

Geographic has ever thrown away a single copy of the magazine, of course, and I think it has been the editors' continuing preoccupation with primitive bare-breastedness that has given the *National Geographic* its unparalleled history of long shelf-life.

There was always the chance that my mother would catch me reading the men's magazines at the drugstore in Newnan, so as a safeguard against this, I would place the copy of *Saga* or *Argosy,* or an occasional *True Detective,* inside a copy of *Boys' Life* or *Progressive Farmer,* as a clever ruse against being found out as some sort of pervert with unsavory desires and interests.

When my friend Danny tapped me on the shoulder that Saturday afternoon before the hayride, I quickly shut the cover of *Boys' Life* around the copy of *Saga,* in which there was a particularly steamy article concerning a sailor's memoirs of shore leave in the South Pacific, complete with black-and-white photographs of the author admiring the fruits of a young native girl.

Danny asked if I had any plans for the evening. My social life at that point was completely stagnant. An exciting night was sitting outside underneath the weeping willow tree with my grandfather, listening for the mail train to Montgomery, or perhaps sitting in on a family butter bean-shelling, which always included conversations about the town's sick and dying.

"Hear about Mavis Spratlin?" my grandmother would ask those assembled. "She went to the hospital last week with cancer. They cut her open, but there was nothing they could do, so they just sewed her right back up."

It appeared to me that every time we shelled butter

beans, somebody had just been to the hospital to be cut open, only to be sewn right back up. I always imagined this scene: The doctor has finished making his incision and is looking into the poor patient's entrails. "No use wasting our time anymore with this poor soul," he says to the nurse. "Let's just sew her right back up and break for lunch."

The only other time there was a change in my otherwise dull, routine evenings was when Billy Graham came on television. That would attract the entire family to the front of the set, and there also would be occasional visitors from other homes who were still without the magic of television, but who were enthralled by the young evangelist from North Carolina. There were two schools of Billy Graham thought in those days. There was, in fact, a minority that felt he was in the business of saving souls for financial gain, and they watched him on television in order to make such knowing comments to the others as, "I hear he's got a big house and two cars, and his wife goes to the beauty parlor twice a week."

The majority of people, however, felt the Lord had purposely provided him with such worldly favors because he was doing such a jam-up job of spreading the Word, and to miss one of his broadcasts on television would have been as sinful as staying home from church on Sunday morning to plow. Harvey Hogan, legend had it, had sent his wife and children off to services alone one Sunday morning, and then had proceeded shamelessly to plow his fields, while his pitiful family sat with heads hung low, listening to the preacher deliver a fitting sermon entitled, "Laying by the Fields of Jesus."

It was only a few weeks afterwards, the story went on, that Harvey's mule took sick and got all bloated up and died a painful, agonizing death, while all Harvey could do was sit and watch. That the Lord would punish the mule, who, given the choice, would have never stood in the way of Harvey's church attendance, bothered me somewhat. If anybody deserved to get bloated up and die, I thought to myself, it was Harvey Hogan, and not his mule. I mentioned that to my grandmother, who promptly quoted something out of St. Matthew that didn't seem to apply to the situation, so I presumed that perhaps the Lord simply had it in for mules, and let it go at that.

By the time I was fourteen, I knew the Billy Graham show by heart. Cliff Barrows would announce that we were all facing the "hour of dee-ci-shun," and then he would say, "Dr. Graham will be with us in a moment, but, first, let's hear a musical salute to our Cre-a-tor from George Beverly Shea."

George Beverly Shea, who looked a great deal like Harvey Hogan, come to think of it, would stand behind the pulpit and do "How Great Thou Art" to a football stadium full of believers and my family and the others gathered around the television in hypnotic wonderment.

When he was finished, my grandmother would say, "He sure can sing, can't he?" And there would be approving nods around the room as the tension mounted with the prospect that Dr. Graham soon would be with us.

I never knew exactly what to make of Billy Graham, but he did frighten me, especially when my grandmother pointed out that the man looked sort of like God. I was never certain exactly how my grandmother was able to focus on this resemblance, since there were no known photographs of the Almighty, but the more I looked at Billy Graham, the more I began to agree that he had the look of deity. I think it was his hair and his eyes. Billy Graham's hair was always swept back, as if it had been styled by some howling wind on a mountaintop, and his eyes were piercing, and they seemed to say Billy knew exactly what he was talking about, and anybody who didn't believe him had better start shopping around for a new mule.

As I stood by the magazine racks in the Newnan drugstore, thinking about Billy Graham's hair, Danny offered me his invitation to the church hayride. I didn't give him a firm answer at the time. Having never been on a hayride before, I wasn't certain it was anything that held any appeal for me. Hay normally made me sneeze and itch. However, when I weighed that option against watching the Billy Graham special that was scheduled for television that very evening, I chose the sneezing and itching of the hay over the sweating and squirming I normally did when Billy Graham looked at me with those eyes, and with a message centering around the fact that we could all expect to hear from Gabriel's horn in the very near future.

What I didn't know was that my cousin Melba had offered her invitation to Paula. Some thirty seconds after the hayride began, the required singing of one verse of "Found a Peanut" behind us, the couples settled into each other's arms in the hay, and there sat me and Paula and the chaperone, with nothing in common except the Book of Timothy.

I moved with great haste. First, I nestled myself between the object of my ever-growing, lustful interest, Paula, and the chaperone, the wife of the young Baptist minister who was happily driving the tractor at the time, completely unaware that he was pulling what amounted to the parking lot of a drive-in movie behind him.

After a few casual remarks to the preacher's wife concerning the unhappy physical state of Mavis Spratlin, I turned my attention to Paula, who was especially stunning that evening and whose Evening in Paris perfume, mixed with the scent of the hay, drove me into a wild sneezing fit. When I recovered, however, I could tell she was warming to me.

"Let me have your coat, Four-Eyes," she said. "I'm freezing to death out here."

I immediately peeled off my jacket, something from my fall ensemble I had bought from Judson Smith, who ran a cut-rate clothing warehouse during the week and auctioned used cars on Saturday nights.

Then I was freezing myself, but I was not about to let a little discomfort keep me from seizing this incredible opportunity that had come my way.

"I hated to miss Billy Graham tonight," I began, through chattering teeth.

"I never watch that," Paula replied. "He spooks me."

I inquired as to whether her family owned a mule and was relieved when she informed me they didn't.

"What's a mule got to do with Billy Graham, anyway?" she asked.

I captured her undivided attention with the Harvey Hogan story, indicating that missing a Billy Graham broadcast did carry with it some risk. Although my family didn't own a mule at that point, either, I went on, I was yet somewhat hesitant to pass up Billy Graham in order to attend the hayride.

"Mules aren't the only things that can bloat up and die, you know," I said, mentioning that my family did own several chickens and one rather busy rooster.

"Then why did you come along on the hayride?" Paula asked.

It was at that point that I learned another valuable lesson about women. If it flatters them enough, they will believe it. Politicians have been using this technique on their constituents for years. Former Georgia governor Eugene Talmadge was a master of it. When the "lying Atlanta newspapers," as he always termed them, implied that he was guilty of misappropriating state funds, Gene went forth into the hinterlands and shouted to the assembled crowds, "They say I stole! Well, maybe I did steal a little, but who did I steal for? I stole for you, my fellow Georgians! I stole for you!"

The crowd, enamored by the fact that their governor thought enough of them to pilfer on their behalf—and never thinking to ask just how *they* had benefited—cheered and cursed the newspapers, and ol' Gene went on about his way.

"Why do you think I came along?" I asked Paula, attempting to whisper above the tractor's grinding engine sounds and the constant smacking caused by the locking and unlocking of thirty pairs of lips around us. "I came because I knew you would be here."

Something golden had finally rolled off my tongue. Years of hatred Paula had built up for me vanished in a matter of seconds. She suddenly had her head resting on my shoulder. I moved my right arm around her, catching two splinters off the side of the wagon in the back of my hand, but ignoring the pain in the midst of such bliss. I might have kissed her for the first time at that very moment, had the Evening in Paris and the hay not gotten to me again, causing another sneezing fit. However, I quickly reached for my handkerchief, gave my nose a couple of quick blows, and drew her close to me again.

"I didn't realize I would make you sneeze," Paula cooed into my ear.

"I always sneeze when I'm falling in love," I said, amazed at my own romantic brilliance, even while attempting to cope with the freezing cold and a running nose.

We drew closer together in the hay, and I could sense she was filled with a longing desire to press her lips against mine. I had never actually kissed a girl in the mouth before. Shirley Ann and I had not reached that plateau. She had heard that if you touched tongues, it could make you have a baby, and my limited knowledge of the biological process had rendered me helpless to convince her otherwise.

This wise young woman in my arms, who had just turned fourteen, knew that if you were careful not to swallow each other's spit, absolutely nothing could happen. So I took a deep breath, swallowed, and bent my head toward hers, extending my neck far beyond its previous limitations, and I took my first kiss, in the dark woods of Coweta County, about a half-mile from Bear Creek, if my estimate of location was correct.

My eyes were closed tightly and my heart was thumping. She held out a slight pucker for me, and I puckered my own lips in order to fit hers perfectly. I was slightly off-target, however, and wound up with my lower lip on the top of her chin. My teeth were continuing to chatter, which was one of my problems, and the fact that we were groping along a rocky, dirt road in a hay wagon made the perfect union of lips even more difficult.

I quickly moved my lips around, however, until I had top-on-top and bottom-on-bottom with Paula's, and we held that first kiss for well over a minute, even though the hay wagon rolled through three mudholes and over what felt like a log in the road as we clutched each other. We might have held the kiss even longer, had we both already mastered the art of kissing and breathing at the same time, but our lack of experience eventually forced us to draw our heads back and gasp for breath. I bumped my head on the side of the wagon as I drew back, taking on more splinters, this time in my scalp. I was oblivious to the pain, however, and once my lungs were filled with the appropriate amount of air, I sought her mouth once more.

How long I had awaited this moment. Years of frustration gave way to unmatched ecstasy. We broke from our clutch only long enough to jump down off the wagon and gulp down a quick hot dog and a marshmallow or two at fireside, when we stopped at Bear Creek. We were the first ones back on the wagon, and we kissed away the entire return trip to the church. I forgot about the cold and the splinters in the back of my hand and in the back of my head. I forgot about the pain of Shirley Ann. I forgot how much I disliked that snake, Willard Haines, for taking her away from me. I forgot about everything and everybody—except Billy Graham.

Had I sinned the ultimate sin? The thought began to creep back inside my consciousness, as the end of the hayride and the end of my first night of intimacy with a member of the opposite sex neared. Could I ever be forgiven for turning away from a Graham broadcast to engage in such pleasures, a waver from righteousness that certainly would bring down the wrath of God on me? So we didn't have a mule. That might make it even worse.

Harvey Hogan had a mule on which God could take out his anger. With no mule in the family, what if God decided to point his finger at me? What if I suddenly bloated up and died? How would I explain that to my grandmother?

The fears grew even worse. What if Paula had swallowed some of my spit? She would get pregnant and have to leave home. Our parents would keep us apart forever, and again I would be banished to nights of listening for the mail train and shelling butter beans, which reminded me of what happened to Mavis Spratlin. What if God were so angry at me that he would make me have cancer? I could hear my grandmother clearly: "Terrible thing about Lewis," she would say, as she threw a handful of butter beans into the sack next to her chair. "They cut him open, but then they just sewed him right back up again."

As the hay wagon was pulled into the churchyard, and as Paula and I pulled away from our final embrace, my emotions were torn between the absolute joy of what had so surprisingly transpired, and the dread that I felt over what price I eventually might have to pay for this delicate, delicious, momentous occasion in my life.

That night, alone and deep under the covers of my bed, I carefully weighed each feeling against the other. I concluded, before dozing off to a myriad of dreams that even *Saga* or *Argosy* wouldn't recreate on their steaming pages, that no matter what God had in store for me as a result of my transgression, a night in the arms of Paula, sweet Paula, would be well worth it a thousand times over

VIII

Sally Was a Good Ol' Girl

another as I settled into deep envy. What of my mind, I would ask myself? Are they not awed each time I rise in English class to give a brilliant explanation of when and where to use a semi-colon? Are they not fetched by my ability to wade through an algebraic puzzle, my hand moving across the blackboard with incredible speed and direction? Are they not impressed with my knowledge of history and geography? Did they not swoon when I deftly handled the instructor's question concerning the mathematical makeup of each house of Congress?

Alas, they did not. First, it was Willard Haines and his car, and now it would be a football player with his muscles.

The dance floor was crowded at the Newnan National Guard Armory, as Buddy Holly sang on records of a love lost in the pouring rain. We had shed our socks and were holding each other close. I knew all the words to the song, and I was singing along in Paula's ear as we two-stepped across the floor, heavy with a new coat of wax.

Suddenly I felt a tapping on my shoulder. Actually, it was more than a tap. What I felt was a large hand pulling me away from my dancing partner. The next instant, I was standing alone on the dance floor in my socks, while Bubba Gatewood, who had made fourteen individual tackles and recovered a fumble in the evening's victory over North Clayton, was dancing away with Paula.

I decided to be a gentleman about the entire situation, and allow them to have a few dances together before breaking back into the arms of my darling. I let them play everything Buddy Holly sang, an entire Johnny Mathis album, a rousing Duane Eddy guitar harangue, and then went and had some punch before I finally decided to take my life in my hands and rescue Paula from Bubba, who outweighed me some eighty pounds.

In my fearful state, however, I tapped Paula on the shoulder instead of Bubba, who always danced the slow dances with his eyes closed. Imagine my horror when Paula, thinking I was another girl who wanted to be in the clutches of Newnan High School's defensive terror, stepped away, and there I stood face-to-face with Bubba Gatewood, who thought I wanted to dance with him, too.

Quick-thinker that I was, however, I was able to escape what would have been a bloody scene by explaining that Paula's mother had just called and wanted her home immediately because of the death of her aunt.

"It was horrible about her aunt, Bubba," I stammered. "They cut her open, but she was in such bad shape by that time, all they could do was just sew her right back up."

Bubba didn't give up that easily, however. The following Sunday evening, I was watching the seals eat fish and honk horns on "The Ed Sullivan Show" when Danny Thompson gave me a call at home.

"I just thought you would like to know," he said. "Bubba Gatewood picked up Paula after BTU and they drove off together."

Once again, I was to be left as a dangling participle in the compound sentence of love. My stomach was a bottomless pit of agony and despair. My mother heard me crying in my room.

"Son," she said softly, "is there anything I can do to help?"

I explained, between sobs, the sorry state of my love life, that I had been pushed aside as Bubba Gatewood would fling an opposing quarterback to the ground.

"I'll squeeze you some fresh orange juice," my mother said, "and you will feel a lot better."

Moments later, she returned with the orange juice. I gulped it down in a couple of swallows. We talked for another hour. We talked of life and love and of the inevitable pitfalls of romance that always befall youth, and she brought me more orange juice, and she stroked my head with her soft hands, and I said to her, "At least you've never left me."

I think I sensed in her at that moment a deep fulfillment, one that mothers who love their sons must crave, must need to satisfy any questions in their own minds concerning their worth as parents. She smiled and put her hands around my head, and she looked into my eyes with tears falling down over her own cheeks, and she said, "No, I've never left you, but one day you will leave me and start your own family. You're getting older, son," she said, "but just promise me you will wait until you're sure. Promise me you won't fall in love too soon and too quickly. If Paula really loves you, she'll come back. But no matter what, take your time. You are hurt now, but you are young, and it will pass before you know it. Later, it won't be that easy to give up people. Just promise me you won't ask me to give you up to somebody else until you are absolutely certain she is what you want."

I knew I could promise her that, because I knew it would take a woman just like her to satisfy me, and no manner of female who could be lured away by the likes of

Bubba Gatewood could ever be depended upon to hand-squeeze orange juice or stroke my head in moments of great despair.

"I promise, mama," I said. And I meant it.

I always have wanted to be able to pout for long periods of time and to be unforgiving to scheming women who did me wrong. I always have wanted to be able to walk away from them with something Clark Gable might have said. I have wanted to listen to their apologies, and then crack open a half-smile and leave them standing in the wake of my indifference.

I have never been able even to come close to doing anything like that. I am, and always have been, a complete pushover when, on those rare occasions, women have asked me to forgive them. They can disarm me with a soft touch or kiss or smile. They can chase away my anger or distrust with a well-placed, "But it's *you* I love, not *him*." And they can always cry. God, I have always hated to see a woman cry. I know it is often a ploy, but when a woman cries, there is something inside me that says, give her whatever it is she wants, at whatever cost.

Paula said she was sorry. "We just rode around," she explained.

"Where did you go?" I asked sternly.

"Just around."

"Did you park anywhere?"

"Of course we didn't park anywhere."

"How long were you out with him?"

"Just two hours. We rode up to Newnan and got an ice cream cone at the Tastee-Freez and then he took me home."

"I thought you said you didn't park."

"We didn't park. Except to get an ice cream."

"Did you kiss him?"

"Of course I didn't kiss him."

"Did he try to kiss you?"

"Of course he tried to kiss me, but I didn't let him."

"Why not?"

"I just didn't."

"You didn't even let him kiss you goodnight?"

"It was just a little kiss."

"How little?"

"Just a little goodnight kiss."

"On the mouth?"

"Sort of on the side."

"He kissed you on the side of your mouth?"

"That's all it was, just a little kiss on the side of my mouth."

"Which side?"

"I don't remember which side it was. Mama left the porch light on. I just let him kiss me that once, and then I went inside."

"What if the porch light hadn't been on? Would you have let him kiss you more than once?"

"Of course I wouldn't have let him kiss me more than once. I just wanted to go for a ride in his car, that's all."

"What kind of car does he have?"

"Impala."

"Stick or automatic?"

"Stick."

"Two-barrel or four?"

"Four."

"Mag wheels?"

"Yes."

"Glass-packs?"

"I think so."

"Did he ask you to go riding around with him again?"

"Yes, but I'm not going."

"Why not?"

"Would you be mad if I went riding around with him again?"

"Why should I be mad? If you want to go riding around with Bubba Gatewood, then that's your business."

"Then why are you mad now?"

"I'm not mad."

"Yes you are."

"I am not."

"Yes you are. When you're mad, your face turns red."

"So my face turns red. Big deal."

"I think it's kind of cute."

"You do?"

"Yeah, your face turns red and you pooch out your bottom lip."

"I don't pooch out my bottom lip."

"Yes you do. You turn red and your bottom lip pooches out, and I think you're really cute."

"Am I cuter than Bubba Gatewood?"

"He's not really that cute up close, and after he ate his ice cream, he started belching."

"He belched?"

"Real loud. It was gross."

"I never belched around you."

"That's something else I like about you. I don't ever

remember you belching during the entire time we've been dating.''

"Belching in front of a girl is gross.''

"That's something else. You're very considerate.''

"I don't have an Impala and I don't play football, though.''

"I don't care about all that. All I want is you.''

"Do you mean that?''

"Of course I mean that. Do you forgive me?''

"I guess so.''

"Do you want to kiss me?''

"Yes.''

"Well, kiss me.''

"You sure you don't remember which side of your mouth Bubba Gatewood kissed you on?''

"Why does it matter?''

"I don't want to touch that spot with my mouth.''

"I promise you'll never have to worry about Bubba Gatewood again.''

"Promise?''

"Promise.''

"I love you.''

"I love you, too.''

*　　　　　*　　　　　*

I turned sixteen on October 20, 1962. I had marked the days off on my calendar for a year. I was the first one in line to take my driver's test at Georgia State Patrol headquarters. When they handed me the piece of paper that made it legal for me to drive any place I wanted to go, anytime, it was a moment of utter joy. The following weekend, I picked up Paula at her house in the family 1958 Pontiac.

Paula lived a mile away from me, down behind Steve Smith's truck stop. Her father was a nice man who drove trucks loaded with new cars. Her mother was a nice lady named Miss Inez, who always left the front porch light on for her only child.

As I drove to Paula's house that first time, I recalled all the other occasions when I had driven up meekly on my bicycle. Miss Inez has always been very kind to me. I think she appreciated the fact that, as long as her daughter was dating a young man who offered no more than a bicycle as transportation, her daughter was safe from harm. I have no statistics to back this up, but I am certain very few young women have ever gotten into the worst of all possible troubles after riding off with a young man on a bicycle.

Miss Inez apparently was concerned, however, about the fact that I appeared undernourished, and whenever I visited her house, she would go to great lengths to feed me.

"Are you hungry?" she would ask, gazing at my pitiful physique.

"No ma'am," I would answer.

"How about a sandwich?"

"No thanks."

"You want some fruit?"

"No thank you."

"How about a piece of cake?"

"I already had dessert."

"Do you want a glass of milk?"

"I'm fine, thank you."

"I have some delicious macaroni and cheese left over from dinner."

"We had macaroni and cheese last night."

I noticed Miss Inez's attitude toward me had changed a bit when I drove up in the Pontiac, however.

"Got your driver's license?" she asked me.

"Last week," I answered.

"Did you do well on the test?"

"Very well."

"You don't drive fast, do you?"

"No ma'am."

"You don't care anything about drag racing, do you? Some of the boys like to drag race. I think it's very dangerous."

"I don't like to drag race. Our car is an automatic anyway."

"You don't want to park, either, do you? Some of the boys take their dates out and they park."

"No ma'am, I would never want to go parking."

"You know where that could lead, don't you?"

"Yes ma'am."

"Where are you taking Paula tonight?"

"I thought we would get something to eat and then go see a movie."

"You're hungry? I've got some macaroni and cheese left over from dinner."

"No thanks. I thought maybe we would go to the Tastee-Freez and get a hamburger."

"You're going to the movie then?"

"Yes ma'am."

"You aren't going to the drive-in, are you? Some of the

boys like to take their dates to the drive-in, but I don't think girls Paula's age should go, do you?''

"No ma'am."

"You know where that could lead, don't you?''

"Yes ma'am."

"I want you to bring Paula home by eleven. Can you bring her home by eleven?''

"Yes ma'am. By eleven."

"How about a piece of fruit?''

"I'll just wait and get a hamburger at the Tastee-Freez.''

With a car, Miss Inez realized that, despite my obvious weak condition from lack of food, I was no longer a little boy on a bicycle. I was a potential lethal weapon.

I am certain most women's sexual hangups that occur later in life come as a direct result of the warnings and advice their mothers gave them before they went off the first time with a boy in his car. There is even, I would discover over the years, a mother's list of commandments of how a daughter should handle herself when she's alone with a boy; the list has been passed down from buggy generations and updated slightly to fit the automotive age.

Roughly, these commandments cover everything from parking to never allowing one's self to be touched anywhere lower than the chin or higher than the ankle, and the all-encompassing directive from a mother to a daughter is, ''Always act as if I were in the car with you, watching everything you're doing.''

Some daughters are haunted by such a restrictive instruction, and are well into their married years before they stop checking closets and under their beds for their mothers before allowing their husbands to make love to them.

A friend even told me of being out with a young coed in college whose mother had convinced her that, no matter where she was, she could never remove herself from her mother's watchful eyes. After several months of dating and gradually getting more daring, a moment of high passion arrived, and as my friend was about to remove certain obstacles standing in the way of his advance—her clothes—the girl screamed out, "Close your eyes, Mama! It's too late to turn back now!"

I forgot all about the hamburgers at the Tastee-Freez the moment I got Paula out of the driveway, and I also forgot my promises to Miss Inez and headed straight for the Newnan Drive-In. Paula and I had double-dated to the drive-in before, but there are certain negative aspects of double-dating at a drive-in movie.

In the first place, the other fellow's date inevitably will want to watch the movie and will carry on a running commentary of what's going on, even if you and your date have no interest in anything but each other.

"Oh, look at that!" she will say, turning to the back seat to get your attention. "Doris Day is so pretty when she wears yellow. Don't you think Doris Day is pretty when she wears yellow?"

Petting, even the lightest forms, deserves the strict, undivided attention of both participants—the hell with Doris Day in yellow, or in any other color for that matter.

The opposite of that situation is when the other couple has far advanced you and your date, and they disappear from view even before the speaker is in the car. This tends to make your date nervous, and it also makes you frustrated to realize that you are a relative newcomer to the drive-in ranks, while the stud in the other seat is obviously a journeyman performer.

Two couples in one car was also more likely to attract Haskel (The Rascal) Pratt, the drive-in security guard who enjoyed nothing more than sneaking up behind your car and flinging open a door and shining a flashlight squarely on the activities taking place on the seats. Haskel got twenty-five dollars a week and all he could see. Double-daters gave him a shot at a two-for-one bonanza.

But finally Paula and I were alone. She wore an orange dress that night and matching lipstick. Doris Day had never looked better. By the middle of the second feature, her lips were blue, however, wounded victims of years of stored-up fantasies and dreams about finally taking my own girl in my own car to a drive-in theater, and clutching her in my arms, and flinging my mouth upon hers.

"You press too hard when you kiss," she said.

"I lost my head," I replied.

"You know why I really never wanted to go out with Bubba Gatewood again?"

"Why?"

"He pressed too hard when he kissed."

"I thought you said he only kissed you on the side of the mouth."

"That's where he ended up. He started on the front and pressed so hard he turned my head sideways, and slipped off my lips and nearly broke my jaw."

"Then it wasn't the belching?"

"Everybody belches now and then."

"I don't."

"Maybe it's because you don't eat enough. Mother has some macaroni and cheese left over...."

I had her home well before eleven. We finished off the macaroni and cheese before we said good night in the glare of Miss Inez's porch light. I kissed her on the cheek. It was two weeks before her lips were well enough to kiss her there again.

Much to my constant chagrin, being able to drive a car wasn't the answer to all my frustrations involving girls. This was the last gasp of the pre-pill era. Occasionally, the scandal of a teen-age pregnancy rocked the community, but such an occurrence was rare, indeed. And after word leaked out that some mother's child had, in fact, turned up pregnant, the chances of anybody else within a fifty-mile radius having the same misfortune befall them were practically nil for six months.

Each mother used the example of the poor, pregnant girl at every opportunity with the constant warning, "Be careful, or you're going to wind up just like Lorna Haygood." Lorna Haygood, the poor thing, was used so often as an example by mothers that her name became synonymous with the entire human sexual experience.

"Anybody been Lorna Haygooding lately?" the boys would ask each other at the Tastee-Freez after taking their dates home.

"You kiddin' me?" somebody answered one night. "If I ever got any Lorna Haygood in this town, I'd put it in the newspaper."

What had happened to Lorna, went the most accepted story, is that she had met a boy from Atlanta who was much older than she, and he had told her that he loved her and that he would marry her when she got out of high school and he got out of the Navy, so she decided to go all the way. Even if she did happen to get pregnant, she could always say they had been married secretly when she was eleven years old, and everybody would, of course, believe her.

When she did get pregnant, however, her boyfriend from Atlanta was off on a ship somewhere, and they had to send poor Lorna to the Florence Crittenton Home for Unwed Mothers.

The spectre of the Florence Crittenton Home hung so heavily over the heads of the girls in my high school, after the Lorna Haygood affair, that it is doubtful that the number of couples actively engaging in anything beyond mouth-to-mouth contact, with an occasional above-the-waist feel, *if* you had discussed becoming engaged after your first year of college, would have filled up a small station wagon. Not only was this terribly frustrating to the eager-to-sow-their-oats young men of the community, but Haskel (the Rascal) Pratt also quit his job at the drive-in and went to work as a sheetrocker.

Paula's firm resolve not to exceed the unspoken, yet firm, standards which the girls of the community had set for themselves (the boys called it their Lorna Haygood Doctrine) took some of the pressure off me. And when Miss Inez gave Paula a certain piece of paper to carry on her person at all times, I knew I would have to look elsewhere for the unspeakable pleasures that I knew had to be out there someplace. The slip of paper, incidentally, had two words on it—"Florence Crittenton." At the drive-in, Paula always took the paper out of her pocketbook at intermission in order to remain strong during the second feature.

There was, however, in our community, as in many others during those years when girls clung fast to their virginity, a certain breed of young women, who, for one reason or another, were much freer with their favors. They probably saved any number of young men from mental breakdowns before their time, in the face of what seemed to be permanent celibacy. I doubt that anyone knows the exact figures, but I would guess that before the pill and the casting-off-of-sexual-bonds by women in the '70s, it was a mere handful of these young women who took care of the desires of millions of American males.

We joked about them, and they would always ask us, "Why do you never call me on the weekends?" And no, they never got invited to Homecoming dances or never were asked to save a last dance at the Key Club Sweetheart Ball. In retrospect, such treatment of them was shameful, but they were special to us, and had we fully realized their worth in the development of our sexual selves, we certainly would have treated them with more respect.

Sally Gladstone was one of those girls. She lived in a trailer park outside of town, third double-wide on the left, and her father worked the night shift and her mother worked the first. Sally could get out anytime she pleased and stay out until all hours. The front of her trailer resembled a taxi stand most nights, as the young callers queued up for a chance to take her on a long drive to Hilley's Mill, or on a short one over behind Robert and Alf's beer joint.

Sally had only two rules. One, you had to use the crude

protection devices of the day, and two, you had to kiss her fifteen minutes first.

"That gets my engines cranked up," Sally used to say. She was no dummy. So eager were most of the boys who took her out, fifteen minutes of kissing Sally Gladstone often meant that her over-eager suitor was no longer in the play for the final act. Premature something-or-other.

My one and only night with Sally is something I will never forget. We drove off deep into the wooded area near Bear Creek, where I first kissed Paula. The hours I had spent thinking of this moment, when I would actually be allowed to solve the feminine "mystery" Loretta Lynn would sing about later in country songs! That I would be taking from a loaf oft-sliced did not bother me in the least. I was, I realize now, violating the first law of sexual intimacy. I was doing this only for myself. Sally was a faceless figure in the dark of the front seat. At that moment, she had no identity. She could have been any of so many Sally Gladstones, who have served their nation through the years.

I stammered and fumbled and considered calling the whole thing off when Sally's hair became entangled in the handle that rolled down the window on the passenger's side of the front seat of the family car. As I attempted to maneuver myself in the total darkness to a position where I could help Sally free her hair and her head, I accidentally hit the horn on the steering wheel with my leg. The resounding honk that blared through the silence of the surrounding woods nearly caused me to have a heart attack. I can only imagine what the possums, raccoons, and hoot owls must have thought.

And Sally's hair was still caught in the door handle. Unable to untangle it by yanking Sally's head a number of times, as she screamed out in pain, I decided to turn the handle to see if that would help. It didn't. All that accomplished was entangling more of Sally's hair.

"First time, huh?" she asked as I fumbled through my glove compartment in search of the owner's manual. Perhaps it would explain how to untangle hair from a window handle.

"Sort of," I said.

"What do you mean, 'sort of?' "

"Well," I tried to explain, "I've given a lot of thought to it."

"Obviously not enough," replied Sally, who now could move her head only a couple of inches in either direction, so tightly was her hair woven around the handle.

Several thoughts raced through my mind. What if I couldn't get her hair out? I would have to drive her home with her head stuck to the side of the door. What if some of my friends were waiting for her at the trailer park? "What did you have to do," they would howl at me, "tie her down first?"

And what if I still couldn't free Sally's head? Would I have to remove the handle? How would I explain that to my mother, when she asked why there was no handle to roll down the window on the passenger's side of the car?

"Well, mother, I was with this girl, and she got her hair caught in the. . . ."

"What was she doing with her head down that far in the seat?" my mother would ask.

"She was a very short girl, mother," I would attempt to explain.

What else was occurring to me at that point was that I was well on my way to totally fouling up my long-awaited first opportunity to perform the ultimate act. None of this was supposed to have happened. We were supposed to have driven into the woods and made love while the possums, raccoons, and hoot owls serenaded us with some passionate rhapsody, the sort of music they always played in the movies to signify the entwined couple was about to engage in something they couldn't show in movies in those days.

I felt the disappointment of a child awakening on Christmas morning to find a toy train under his tree, only to discover that Santa had forgotten the batteries. I wanted to start this whole thing over. I wanted all of this to be erased, and I wanted to be back at the trailer park, picking up Sally. I would suggest that she wear a cap or other cover to keep her hair from getting tangled in the window handle, and I would move smoothly to her, covering her face with fire-starting kisses, and then. . . .

And then I realized there was only one way I would ever get Sally Gladstone's head freed from the window handle on my door, and that was to cut her hair off with a pair of scissors. Since neither of us had such an instrument, I further realized that if I were to satisfy my lust this night I would have to do it with the lustee's head rendered basically immobile.

"Can you do it like this?" I selfishly asked her.

"I'll try," said Sally, sport that she was.

It was over in a matter of seconds, much to Sally's

relief. Any attempt at movement on her part brought a cry of anguish, as the door handle yanked violently at her hair. The experience hadn't been exactly what I had expected, but I suppose any port would have been welcome in that rather embarrassing and frustrating storm.

I cranked the car and drove out of the woods with Sally's head still attached to the door. Locating a pair of scissors at ten o'clock in the evening was a definite problem. I couldn't go home with Sally Gladstone sprawled out in the front seat of my car, and we couldn't go back to the trailer park until her head was freed, either, lest I be the subject of much ridicule and scorn.

My only hope was that Carla, the night waitress at Steve Smith's truck stop in Moreland, might have a pair of scissors in her pocketbook. It was a long shot, but I had no other choice.

"What in the world do you need a pair of scissors for at this time of night?" Carla, serving coffee to a couple of truckers, asked me.

"You wouldn't believe me if I told you," I said. "Just see if you have a pair of scissors."

She didn't. However, one of the truckers overheard our conversation and said he had a pair of wirecutters in the cab of his truck. I promised I would need them for only a couple of seconds.

Wirecutters are just the ticket for removing a girl's head from a car door. A couple of clips, and Sally was upright again for the first time in more than an hour.

"How do you feel?" I asked her.

"My neck hurts and I'm dizzy," she said.

"You aren't going to throw up, are you?" I asked.

That's all I would have needed. First, there is still a patch of blonde hair in the window handle of my car, and now she's going to throw up on the seat covers. Maybe I could drive the car into Bear Creek and start a new life in another town, I thought to myself.

"Get me a Dr. Pepper and some French fries," said Sally. "That will make me feel better."

I went back inside and gave the trucker his wirecutters, and ordered a Dr. Pepper and some French fries from Carla, who was becoming quite suspicious.

"You aren't doing anything weird out there in that car, are you?" she asked me.

I ignored her question. There was no way to explain the sudden need for a pair of scissors, a bottle of Dr. Pepper, and an order of French fries to anybody, much less to a truck stop waitress.

Sally nursed the drink and ate the fries, and I tuned in WLAC in Nashville as we drove back to the trailer park. Jimmy Reed was moaning "Big Boss Man," and I was feeling somewhat better about the entire situation.

I suddenly felt the need to apologize to Sally.

"I'm sorry," I said.

"For what?"

"For fouling up everything."

"It's always that way the first time," she said. "You'll get better at it."

"Would you give me a second chance?" I asked timidly.

She rubbed the bald spot on the back of her head and gave me a vague answer about calling her in a couple of months. I felt terribly sorry for Sally at that moment, not only about what I had put her through, but for what everybody else put her through, too.

Somehow, my youthful mind realized how she was being used, how she was obviously starved for attention, how the only way she knew to get that attention was by servicing half the county. I wondered to myself if anybody would ever really love her, if she could ever find one person to take her someplace besides the drive-in and the woods. I asked her for a swig of the Dr. Pepper. I suddenly felt a little sick at my stomach.

When we drove into the trailer park, a group of boys sat on the hood of a car, anxiously awaiting her return.

"Hey, Sally!" one said as she got out of the car. "What took you so long?"

Oh, my God, I thought. She's going to tell them how I botched everything up.

Sally looked at me. I pleaded with my eyes.

"It takes a little longer with a *man*," she said, smiling at me as she walked inside the double-wide and locked the door behind her.

I drove to an all-night service station after leaving the trailer park, borrowed a screwdriver, and took the window handle off the door of my car and removed the hair Sally had left behind. I rolled it into a tiny ball and put it in my pocket and kept it for a long time. I never called Sally again, but sometimes I would take out the lock of her hair in the privacy of my room, and I would touch it and think of her and wonder why she had done what she had done for me.

I heard later that her father came home one Saturday night drunk and called her all sorts of names, and beat her up pretty badly. After that, she moved out of town and nobody knew exactly where she went.

Maybe she finally did find somebody to love her, I thought. But, more likely, she didn't. Like the song said, Sally was a good ol' girl, Sally was a good ol' girl. But good ol' girls fade into tired old women, having never danced a last dance.

IX

She Wore Spaghetti, But I Loved Her Anyway

PAULA NEVER LOOKED more beautiful to me than she did the night of the Key Club Sweetheart Ball at the Newnan Country Club. Neither of us had ever been inside the Newnan Country Club before. I wore a rented tuxedo. My mother had helped me get into it. The cummerbund seemed a senseless, uncomfortable addendum to the outfit, but if I found it in the bag, I put it on.

Paula wore a red dress, only it was no ordinary red dress. It was bright and it clung to her seventeen-year-old form as if her Maker had picked it out Himself. When we walked into the club, she turned every head. I almost came out of my cummerbund with pride.

We had a band from Atlanta for the dance, the social highlight of this, our senior year, and they played our songs—Elvis, and Maurice Williams and the Zodiacks, and some Marvin Gaye before he went funky. And when they slowed down the tempo and played the Platters' "Only You," I took Paula in my arms, pressed her close to me, shut my eyes, and loved her as I never had before. The fact that Bubba Gatewood had left town after graduating a couple of years earlier allowed me to relax fully into my romantic trance.

From that awkward sixth-grader, Paula had grown into a beauty of a young woman, tall, slender, and graceful with eyes that promised more than I would allow myself to imagine. She was funny; she was sweet. Paula listened to my troubles and, after that awful Bubba Gatewood affair, she rarely gave me any reason to be jealous. I, on the other hand, had a few less-than-notable flings, but they were disturbing to her, nonetheless. After each one, she forgave me and took me back again. There were times when I felt torn between the desire to approach other girls in this, the springtime of my life, and the realization that to do so would be to run the awful risk of losing Paula. This, I would later learn, is a built-in frustration for many men. They want the tender security monogamy offers, but the thrill of the chase and the ego-building catch of the extra-curricular is a powerful magnet that tempts them to stray.

As Paula and I neared graduation, I knew one of two things would have to happen. I was going off to college. She wasn't. Either that distance would put an end to our ever-growing relationship, or it would cement it even further. What I actually had in mind was running college girls all week and seeing my hometown honey on the weekends, but I wasn't honest enough with myself at that age to admit it.

Paula moved to Atlanta after graduation and took a job in a bank. Nights she would attend modeling school, and there could be no doubt that, with her looks and grace and style, she could forge herself a career. I got a job in an Atlanta bank and planned to spend my summer with her, before leaving for college in the fall.

Three friends and I shared a duplex apartment on Sixth Street in Atlanta. Our landlord was a brazen homosexual. The woman who had the other apartment in the duplex didn't get out very much during the day, but she had callers arriving most of the night. We were country boys, basically. It took us several weeks to figure out she wasn't running an all-night pizza joint.

Her name was Barbara. She was perhaps thirty and quite attractive. The four of us spent countless hours thinking about exactly what four, male, recent high school graduates would think about if they lived in an apartment next door to the first, real, live prostitute they had ever seen.

Our questions were many. The most important, of course, was how much she charged. Ronnie Jenkins, who, if everything he told us was true, ranked first in our foursome in number of times having actually done it, figured she would charge at least fifty dollars, maybe even seventy-five.

Either figure was far out of our price range, of course, so Ronnie suggested that we go to her with the offer of a package deal. We would all throw in thirty dollars each, and Ronnie, always the schemer, suggested we possibly could throw in parking cars for the visitors who came to see her at night, as additional payment.

One afternoon, our courage built on the foundation of three beers each, we knocked on her door. Ronnie was our spokesman.

"Barbara," he began, "I hope you will not be offended by this proposal, but you are looking at four young men alone in this large city, far away from our mothers and loved ones for the first times in our lives.

"We all have our high school diplomas, we have good jobs, and all of us will be entering institutions of higher learning in the fall. One of us even plans to go to Vanderbilt and become a lawyer.

"I am sure that you know—in fact, I am *quite* sure that you know—that it is natural for young men, such as ourselves, occasionally to want the companionship of a member of the the feminine gender. And it is that natural desire that has brought us to you. Knowing the nature of your profession, we, however, would never imply that seeking any sort of favors from you would come without a price. Therefore, we are prepared to offer you thirty dollars each—one hundred and twenty dollars total—and we would also agree to pay you in advance. We anxiously await your reply."

I was so caught up in Ronnie's eloquent speech that I had failed to notice that a large man had appeared from somewhere inside Barbara's apartment. He wore sunglasses and his jaw was set tight.

"What is it you punks want?" he asked us.

We waited for Ronnie to think of something brilliant

to say. For once in his life, however, he was speechless.

"They want it for thirty dollars apiece," Barbara said to the man.

He laughed. It was a deep, hollow laugh, the kind a man laughs just before he decides to break the heads of four punks.

"She gets five hundred," said the man. "You punks got five hundred?"

"Dollars?" asked Ronnie, his amazement at the high cost of love in the big city showing in his voice.

"You punks get away from this door, and I don't want to never see you messing about here disturbing my woman again," said the man.

"Sir," said Ronnie, "you can rest assured that you have our word that we will never, never. . . ."

"Shut it, bigmouth," interrupted the man.

I grabbed Ronnie before he apologized our way into the hospital, and we all returned to the sanctity of our side of the duplex. When we felt it was safe to go out again, we went for more beer.

Later in the evening, I asked Ronnie if he would ever think of paying a woman five hundred dollars to make love to her.

"No woman is worth that kind of money," he said.

"How about Ursula Andress?"

"No way."

"Rhonda Fleming?"

"Nope."

"How about an entire night with Dorothy Malone?"

"The whole night?"

"Yeah."

"I don't know. That's still steep."

Sometime in the wee hours, Ronnie came into my room and awakened me.

'I think I would do it," he said.

'What?''

'Pay five hundred dollars for the whole night with Dorothy Malone."

'Why are you telling me this now?'' I asked him.

"I figured I could sell my car and raise four-fifty. Would you lend me the rest?''

'If you could have Dorothy Malone for the entire night, I'd lend you the fifty," I said.

'I knew you would," he replied.

'Think you can go to sleep now?'' I asked him.

'Yeah,'' he said. "I just couldn't go to sleep knowing I was only fifty bucks away from Dorothy Malone.''

I think I understood what he meant by that.

*   *   *

My first two years at the University of Georgia passed quickly. I pledged Sigma Pi fraternity in the fall of my freshman year. I was initiated in the middle of winter quarter, and they showed me the secret handshake.

There was a coed here and there, but again, nobody who could make me forget Paula in Atlanta. Her modeling career was moving rapidly. She wore new makeup and new clothes, and there was an air of sophistication to her now. She also had become a blonde. I liked the new color of her hair. I would catch myself twirling it between my fingers as I had my mother's.

"Why do you always do my hair that way?" she would ask me.

"Feels good in my fingers," I would lie.

I wasn't about to tell her I toyed with her hair because I used to do my mother's hair the same way. Never compare a woman to your mother in any way. This is especially true in the area of food.

You tell a woman you don't like the way she cooked your eggs.

"What's wrong with the way I cooked your eggs?" she will reply.

"They just don't taste right," you continue. "And my mother's eggs never ran all over the plate like these."

The next sound you hear will be in the form of angry screams. The rule is, even if your eggs are running all over the plate when your mother's didn't, eat them anyway. Your mother wouldn't hit you over the head with a frying pan, either, but don't be too sure about a woman who has just finished second in an egg-cooking contest with some ungrateful klutz's mother.

I saw Paula on most weekends. Either I would drive over to Atlanta, or she would visit me in Athens at the university. The Sigma Pi annual spring outing was scheduled in Atlanta my freshman year. We had Jerry Butler for the Saturday night formal at the finest hotel in town, the Atlanta Cabana.

In the afternoon, we all gathered in one of the brother's rooms and began to drink. Paula had never been much of a drinker. Miss Inez, her mother, had instilled a fear of the evils of alcohol in her, but she'd been away from home for a time, and so she gunned down the Jack Black and Coke with the rest of us. She got so smashed, she gave one of my fraternity brothers the secret handshake I had shown her in a moment of weakness several weeks earlier.

"We'll bring this up at the next meeting," said the brother.

Before the dance, we all dressed and went out for dinner. Paula wore a long white dress that somebody else's date helped her get into. She was barely coherent at this point from the many Jack Black and Cokes. At dinner, she ordered spaghetti with meat balls. A few moments after it was placed before her, she went down into the spaghetti, head first.

"What are you doing?" I asked her.

"Taking a little nap," she said, spaghetti covering her face and her hair and dripping down onto her white dress.

I managed to get her face out of her dinner, and the waiter brought a towel to wipe the spaghetti off her. I took her back to her room, while everybody else was listening and dancing to Jerry Butler, and I helped her out of her clothes, and I took her in the bathroom where she, as was the term of the day, called Ralph and Huey long-distance for some thirty minutes. I thought she was going to die, and, I am certain, so did she. She recovered enough to lie down on the bed, but not enough to make it to the dance. I thought of leaving her there and going to the dance by myself. It wasn't every night you got to hear Jerry Butler.

But something stopped me. She nestled into my arms and slept. As I lay there, holding her aching head, some memories crept back, memories from my childhood. It felt good holding a woman that way. It made me feel strong. It made me feel she could depend on me. It made me feel I never wanted to be far away from her again.

Somehow, I had imagined it would be different from this, the moment that I realized there was no reason to look any further for a lifelong companion, the moment I pledged an undying allegiance to the woman in my presence. I always imagined I would be Troy Donahue, and she Sandra Dee, and there would be a soft moonglow upon us, and we would be standing on a beach, the waves crashing around us. A crescendo of violins would play the background music as we embraced. We would drop our champagne glasses onto the sand, and I would pull her close to me, her hair blowing in the ocean's breeze, her lips eager and parted slightly, and a far distant bell would toll, signaling this celebration of love.

Instead of a moonglow, however, we had the flicking light from the television set. I seem to recall the program was "Oh, Susannah," starring Gale Storm and Zasu Pitts. I wasn't Troy Donahue at all. I was some skinny kind from Moreland, Georgia, with thick glasses. Paula could have been Sandra Dee, I suppose, but Sandra Dee probably never fell into her spaghetti or threw up in a motel room. And there were no violins, nor waves crashing, nor bells tolling. Besides the television, all I could hear was the commode running and Paula snoring.

But this is no movie, I thought to myself. This is the reality of a young man totally accepting his love for another, agreeing with himself to love her always and above all others. I loved her enough, I knew then, to break any ties or promises that stood in the way of our inevitable union.

With the symphony playing around me—the commode running, Paula snoring, and Zasu Pitts blabbering—I drifted away to join her in sleep. My last thoughts were of my father. I wondered if he had felt this way about my mother, if there had come that keen moment, when all question of ever being without her had left him. And if he had, how could he have ever allowed her to get away? Why hadn't he fought harder to keep her? How did he sleep nights, knowing that she shared a bed and a life with another man? None of that would ever happen to me, I said to myself. I realized I carried some feelings of inferiority to my father, he, the hero of war. As with any son, there had always been an urgency in me to emulate my father's accomplishments, or even to surpass them. But I knew enough about myself to realize that even if the opportunity to match him as a soldier came to me, I likely would not have the courage nor the strength to follow his lead. But as a husband and father, I said to myself, I could stand above him, and I *would* stand above him. Where he had failed, I would flourish.

Before I slept, I promised myself that. Though she didn't hear me, I promised Paula, too.

*   *   *

We planned the marriage for a year. I had finished my sophomore year at Georgia, and Paula had completed her modeling school, and, in the meantime, some yo-yo had asked her to go off to Gatlinburg with him to model some of his sweaters, forcing me into fits of jealousy and further instilling in me the desire to make it official that she was off the open market.

The big problem, I had thought, would be my mother. The one great fear in her life was that I would not finish college, and she considered early marriages certainly detrimental toward that end. And I had promised her I would not rush toward the altar, and I had meant it at the time, but I had made that promise under duress—Bubba Gatewood was out somewhere, riding around in his car with my girlfriend. I saw no use delaying the inevitable.

I was home for a weekend. My mother was in the kitchen cooking my favorite meal—fried corned beef out of a can, navy beans, cornbread, and French fries. I walked into the kitchen. I was nervous.

"I've got something to tell you," I said.

Mothers know. Somehow, they just know. There was no reason for her to speak. I could see in her face and in her eyes that she was anticipating a momentous, and perhaps dreaded, announcement from me.

She walked to the kitchen table and sat down. Perspiration was running off her forehead from standing over the heat of the stove. I sat across the table from her.

"Paula and I want to get married," I said.

Our eyes were locked together. I thought I read her clearly. She had known this was coming, she was saying to herself. She realized the impatience of youth, but if only they really knew what they were doing, if only there were some way she could tell me, tell us both, that we had so much time yet to go; if only she could make us aware of the dangers and the risk; if only there were something she could say to make us change our minds.

I had dreaded this, and I had already played the scene over in my mind a thousand times.

"You promised me you wouldn't rush into anything like this," she would say.

"I know," I would reply, "but I miss Paula so much, and this turkey asked her to go to Gatlinburg with him, and I just can't wait any longer."

"But what about school?" she would ask.

"I'll finish," would be my answer. "I've got a job, and Paula will get a job, and I'll stay in school."

"She's not pregnant, is she?"

"Of course she's not pregnant. We just love each other very much, and we want to be together."

"You're sure?"

"I'm sure."

"But you're both so young."

"We're nineteen."

"You're making a horrible mistake, son," my mother would continue, beginning to sob. I would feel awful about breaking my promise to her, about disappointing her. I wondered if she would come to the wedding.

The scene, however, was nothing like that at all. My mother and I had both grown out of the protective role she had played in our relationship before. She had given generously, and I had taken, a great deal of independence. We had remained close, but she had not fought against her emptied nest.

As a matter of fact, she had begun to prepare me for life out from under her most comforting wing long before I first took flight. She had allowed me the freedom to make a certain amount of my own decisions. She had, more than anything else, given me her trust. I had abused it at times, but never so much as to cause her to take it away. It was because I knew of that trust, and cherished it so much and appreciated it so much, that I had guarded myself against any intense violation of it. Simply put, the primary reason I never stole a hubcap in my life was because I knew it would have broken my mother's heart.

Now I sat before her, having made the most important decision of my young life, and I had underestimated that precious trust. I had not acknowledged the fact that this woman, my mother, was also my friend, and that her love for me would not allow her to come down hard on me for any decision I made. To have done so would have violated that relationship we had grown to—one of mutual respect, one of understanding. I had no way of knowing it at the time, but to have reached that peak of comfortable interaction with my mother was a monumental happenstance, one that few are ever able to achieve with any other person, much less with a parent.

I sat before her, the result of her raising. She would only bless my decision. The little boy who had bound himself so closely to her, when all around him had seemed so unsettled and temporary, had found himself another attachment. She let him go without the slightest resistance.

We talked about when and where the wedding would take place. We talked about who we would invite. We talked about some old times.

"How did you and daddy decide to get married?" I asked her.

"I thought he would never ask me," she said.

"Were you happy when he did?"

"I didn't sleep for a week."

"You must have loved each other a lot."

"We did. He was always laughing, and your daddy was a handsome man. He had that black, curly hair."

"Do you ever still miss him?"

"When you really love somebody, it never really goes away, even if they do. You have to learn to accept it."

"I'll never leave Paula."

"Don't, son," said my mother.

*   *   *

Ronnie Jenkins, my best man, was not altogether in favor of the marriage. He pointed out to me that once women are married to you, they are no longer quite as understanding about your engaging in such activities as staying out until the wee hours drinking beer, or taking off for the beach on a moment's notice, with five bucks in your pocket, two six-packs iced down in the backseat, and visions of bikini-clad, steel-bellied coeds dancing in your head.

Ronnie also pointed out to me the "erosion factor" concerning women.

"Women," said my best man, "have a way of eroding on you after you marry them."

"How's that?" I asked.

"You know what I mean. You remember Helen Shankles?"

"The girl in high school with the big wazoos?" I asked.

"The same one," said Ronnie. "She got married, and in two years, her backside looked like a double-wide mobile home. After you marry a woman, she knows she's got you, and so she just lets herself go, and she erodes into something that would scare a dog off a meat wagon. Of course, some of them are pretty well eat up even before you marry them.''

I promised Ronnie I would watch for the first sign of any eroding on Paula's part. He still wasn't completely convinced, however.

"You've still got a few hours to change your mind," he said. "We could be three hundred miles away from here before they got everybody quieted down enough to start looking for us.''

I was not without some doubts, of course. There were still times on campus when something lovely in a sun dress would smile at me, and I would thrill at her notice. There had even been a coed I sat next to in one of my classes, and we had gone out for beer one afternoon at Harry's during spring quarter, and the night had found us intertwined at the Alps Road Drive-In. She had given evidence that come fall quarter, I could expect her to be just as cooperative, and perhaps even more so. But, I reasoned, marriage quickly redirects lust into one direction, and any desires for such future involvements simply disappear when the golden band of commitment is placed on a finger.

I had invited four of my fraternity brothers to act as ushers at the Sunday wedding. On Saturday night, we all gathered at my home while the bridesmaids spent the night with Paula. My great concern was how my mother would take the idea of a group of nineteen-year-olds drinking beer in her living room. I explained my concern to H.B., my stepfather, who had a taste for an occasional cold one himself.

"Don't worry about it," H.B. said. "When your mother goes to bed, we'll all have a few beers.''

My mother had never been that intolerant of alcohol and, when she was younger, would even partake herself. But in that place and time, drinking was basically a male exercise, to be conducted mostly outside of the home, in Moose Clubs and Veterans Clubs, and in what we called beer joints—the Deep South version of the neighborhood tavern. An enlightened woman like my mother tolerated the menfolk downing a few in those days, but they rarely joined in. As a matter of act, it was considered somewhat boorish behavior even to drink in front of a woman. When the company was mixed, the men normally would slip off into the kitchen and pop down a quick shot, and then return to the ladies in the parlor, who would pretend they had no earthly idea what was transpiring.

I had no desire to push these traditions, so I went along with my stepfather's plan. As soon as my mother went to bed the night before my wedding, he led my friends and me to the laundry room, where he had iced down several cases of Pabst Blue Ribbon in the washing machine. We went through that rather hastily, and the conversation drifted toward where we could find more beer.

Suddenly, my mother appeared in her robe and slippers in the hallway outside the living room, where the half-dozen of us sat in various states of inebriation. I expected an explosion of some sort, I suppose, even a denouncement of our activity with a biblical allusion. (See, "A drunkard shall not enter the Kingdom of Heaven.")

Instead, my mother summoned me into the hallway and pressed a twenty-dollar bill into my hand. "Here's some money," she said. "You're probably going to need more beer."

I never underestimated the woman again.

*   *   *

Paula and I were married on July 17, 1966, at the little Moreland Methodist Church where my mother had married my stepfather. We kneeled together and I took her hand. The preacher asked the Lord to look over us, and when we stood up again, Paula was my wife.

X

Panty Hose on the Shower Rod and Raisins in the Rice

YOU GOT WHAT?" asked the sultry young coed with whom I had been involved at the Alps Road Drive-In the previous spring.

"Married," I said, in a surprisingly timid manner. Classes had begun for my junior year at Georgia. I was quite proud of my wedding band. It made me feel very adult. Every time I looked at it, I thought of Paula. Why, then, was I acting like I had done something foolish?

"You're a fool," said the coed.

"I love my wife," I said.

"Is she pregnant?"

"No, she isn't pregnant."

"Then why did you marry her?"

"I told you, I love her."

"That's no reason to marry her."

"It's not?"

'Of course it's not. How old are you, anyway?''

"Nineteen."

"Nineteen? You are a fool. I sat around all summer waiting for fall quarter to see you again, and you go off and get married."

I put my hand, the one with the ring, into my pocket.

"You're going to miss out on a lot," said the coed. Ronnie Jenkins had said the same thing. I suddenly felt a little sick to my stomach.

We took a small apartment after we were married. I had a night job. She worked days. We met for lunch each day at our apartment. We ate a lot of frozen fish sticks.

I hadn't counted on a couple of things that happened after I got married. One, there were suddenly opportunities that had never presented themselves before. Where were all of these young women, who suddenly seemed quite interested in me, *before* I got married? Perhaps they thought I was harmless now, or perhaps it is the nature of the female in heat to tease the chained male.

There was this blonde in my political science class, for example. She had the face of an angel and a body that bedeviled my imagination. We had been assigned seats next to one another in the classroom. She smiled at me. She asked me if she could borrow my extra pen. I think our hands may have touched when I handed it to her. I watched her mouth. Sometimes she would lick her lips. I think she did that just for me. When she crossed her legs, she took her time doing it. I think she did that for me, too.

It was obvious she was enchanted by me, and I broke out in a cold sweat each time I looked at, or thought about, her.

Oh, what I could do with this vision of loveliness, I thought to myself. But where had she been all last year and the year before? For two years of college, I'd been surrounded by nothing but Home Ec majors who made their own clothes, and female flute players with hairy legs. So I go off and get married, and what happens? An obviously hot-to-trot thoroughbred is asking me to borrow a pen.

A new girl came to work. She had the dark eyes of a gypsy. She began to flirt with me shamelessly.

"What time is it?" she asked me one night in a low, sexy whisper.

"Quarter to nine," I replied, looking squarely into her deep, black eyes.

"That late, huh?" she said, in an obvious come-on.

The frustration began to build in me. Maybe I had been a fool to get married. I was only nineteen, for God's sake. Everywhere I looked, there was some supple young thing licking her lips, or asking me for the time, and what could I do about it?

Something else I hadn't counted on was "The Dating Game." I had seen the program on television before, but I considered it somewhat mindless. They bring out this honey and she asks questions of three bachelors behind a curtain. One is usually an aspiring actor who is currently a waiter, another parks cars and plans to be a brain surgeon, and the third is majoring in ceramics at UCLA. The girl, a former high school majorette who is into house plants and

Rod McKuen, is supposed to pick the bachelor she would most like to date from the answers she gets to her questions.

After I married, "The Dating Game" took on a special meaning for me. I would watch it each morning before class and soon came to feel cheated, somehow, that I was no longer eligible to sit behind the curtain and be in the running for a free trip to Catalina with a former high school majorette. It wasn't that I really had any desire to appear on "The Dating Game," but the fact that I had already given up my eligibility as a bachelor, with very little fight, annoyed me. I would even pretend I was a candidate.

"Bachelor No. 1 [me]," the announcer would begin, "is a college student at the University of Georgia, majoring in journalism. He enjoys dogs, drinking beer with his friends, and Merle Haggard."

"Bachelor No. 1," my potential date would ask, "what do you consider the perfect date?"

"Drinking beer, listening to Merle Haggard, and petting my dog while you scratch my back," I would answer. She would choose me because I obviously was the artistic type, and off we'd go on a Catalina holiday.

I must have watched five hundred "Dating Game" programs the last two years I was in college. That's five hundred cutie-pies wasting their time with five hundred bimbo waiters who want to become actors, when they could have been off with me, scratching my back, if I hadn't gotten married.

There were also my single friends to deal with. Every

time I ran into one of them on campus, the conversation would be the same.

"So, how's married life?" they would ask me.

"Just great," I would answer them. "How's it going for you?"

"You wouldn't believe it. The other night I had a date with this Phi Mu, and we went out to the Alps Road Drive-In, and when I came back with the popcorn, she had already taken off her. . . ."

They never spared me any of the details of their romantic conquests. The sexual revolution was beginning, and while the rebels stormed the palace, I was strapped on the rack in the dungeon of marriage.

I had been terribly wrong when I thought that going through a wedding ceremony and putting a ring on my finger would take away my desire for further pursuit of the opposite sex. Even with a mouthful of wedding cake, I had the same biological drives I had the day before. Just because I had gone and gotten myself married, I realized, didn't mean I would no longer be interested in something that wiggled poetically when it walked away from me.

Again, the old dilemma came back. I *did* love my wife, but Lord, look coming there, all pink and perfumed! Getting married not only hadn't cooled the temperature of my blood, it had actually raised it. There is nothing more hot-blooded than that same chained dog who can yet sniff the aroma of love, but can't do anything more than that.

There were some other problems involved with being married, too, things I had never considered, having never lived with a woman other than my mother.

There was the pouting phenomenon, for instance. Women are geniuses when it comes to pouting. As I mentioned, I can pout only for a short period of time, and then I finally have to unleash my anger and bring the entire matter out into the open.

Women can pout for hours at a time. You know something is wrong; you know she is angry, but women antagonize you by making you beg them to indicate what's wrong. The following is typical of a pouting woman:

"Hi, honey."

Silence.

"I said, 'Hi, honey.'"

More silence.

"Is there something wrong?"

Not a sound.

"I know something's the matter. What's bothering you?"

"Nothing," she finally says.

"Well, if nothing's wrong, why are you pouting?"

"I'm not pouting."

"Yes, you are. Whenever you say nothing is wrong, that's when I know something is wrong."

"There is nothing wrong; now, leave me alone."

"Is it something I said?"

"It's nothing you said."

"Is it something I did?"

"It's nothing you did."

The man's mind, of course, is racing all the time. What on earth did I do? he asks himself. Did I forget her birthday? Our anniversary? Is it Christmas Eve and I didn't bring home any presents? Did she smell perfume on one of my shirts? Did a strange women call and ask for me?

Usually, it's nothing that severe. It's something quite

small in the man's scheme of things, as a matter of fact, but women have an entirely different set of priorities from men. The conversation continues:

"Well, if it's nothing I said or nothing I did, what on earth are you mad about?"

"I told you I wasn't mad. It was something you didn't do."

"Something I didn't do? What didn't I do?"

"You didn't notice my hair."

"I always notice your hair. You have nice hair."

"If you always noticed my hair, you would have noticed how I've changed it."

"You've changed your hair?"

"I had it cut."

"Well, now that you mention it, it does look shorter in the back."

"I didn't have any cut off the back; I had some cut off the front."

"I'm sorry, sweetheart, it's just that I've had a lot on my mind and. . . ."

"You don't love me."

"Of course, I love you."

"No, you don't."

"Honey, sweetheart, baby, I do love you. Why don't we go out for dinner?"

Taking your wife out to dinner to get her to stop being mad at you often works. However, many women will decide to wait until you have taken them out to dinner to start pouting again. That works this way:

"This is really a nice place. What are you hungry for, darling?"

"I don't want anything to eat."

"What do you mean, you don't want anything to eat? We haven't been out to dinner in a month, and you don't want anything to eat?"

"I'm not hungry."

"I know what it is. You're still mad, aren't you?"

"I am not mad. I'm just not hungry."

"Is it something I said?"

Etc.

Arguing with a woman in a restaurant can drive a man crazy. If you were home, you could bang on the table with your fists and scream to the top of your lungs, in order to make your salient points. In a restaurant, however, a man must control his anger, so as not to draw the attention of the other customers. This makes it necessary to scream at the woman across the table in a whisper, and to clench your napkin in one hand and your water glass in the other in order to keep your fists from banging on the table. Holding back the desire to scream and beat on things will then make a man very red in the face, and that is probably what leads to most of the heart attacks that men have. Women realize this, and that is why they pout in restaurants to begin with.

If you subsequently become angry, they often will stand up out of their chair, toss their napkins angrily on the table, and stalk off to the restroom. And there you sit, like a red-faced idiot, having to deal with the stares of the other customers and the obsequious waiter.

"Hi, I'm Harold," he announces, "and I'll be your waiter this evening."

That makes you even madder. You knew all along he

was the waiter, or he wouldn't have been standing there wearing an apron with a menu in his hands, and you couldn't care less what his name is at a time like this.

"Are you ready to order, sir?" he asks coolly.

"Steak, medium well."

"And will the lady be dining this evening?"

That is to say, is your wife coming back from the toilet, or is she going to stay in there and pout while you eat?

"She'll have Veal Oscar," you say, to avoid any further embarrassment.

Naturally, your wife will come back from the toilet eventually, and when she does and the waiter brings the Veal Oscar, she will say, "Why did you order this for me? I told you I wasn't hungry."

"You had to eat something."

"I don't have to eat if I don't want to eat. What is this mess, anyway?"

"Veal Oscar."

"I hate veal."

"I thought you loved veal."

"You obviously have me mixed up with someone else. Who else have you been taking out to dinner?"

"Are you crazy? I haven't taken anyone else out to din. . . ."

"And would either of you care to see a dessert menu?" interrupts Harold, who has been watching the entire fight from behind a plant and has waited until the inevitable adultery charge, which always comes in a restaurant argument between a man and his wife, to stick his nose into the fray.

What usually happens is that you get indigestion from

eating a steak in the middle of a fit of anger, Harold glares at you as you leave the restaurant because you gave him what you considered to be the appropriate tip—"Never go out in the rain without your overshoes, Harold"—and your wife keeps you awake all night tossing and turning in the bed, because she continued to refuse to eat her Veal Oscar and now she's having hunger pangs. All that, and on the way home, she finally tells you why she was pouting in the first place—you forgot it was the fifth anniversary of the first time you kissed, which was behind the windmill hole the night you took her on a date to play miniature golf.

Crying, of course, is the ultimate female weapon. As they will not admit they are pouting, neither will they admit that the clear liquid running down their face and smearing mascara on their cheeks is actually tears.

"Why are you crying?"

"I'm not crying."

"Yes, you are. I can see you are crying."

"I don't know how you can see me crying if you don't notice anything else about me."

Check quickly. Hair? No. She's lost weight? No. She's wearing a new shade of lipstick? No. She's had the earring holes in her ears plugged back up? Not that, either.

"Give me a hint."

"If you don't know what I'm talking about, it's no use to give you a hint."

That, of course, makes no sense whatsoever, but when a woman is crying, nothing she says or does will make any sense.

"Okay, I give up. Please tell me what I didn't notice."

"I turned the bed in a different direction, and you've slept in it three nights and haven't noticed."

Dandruff, large snarling dogs, thunderstorms, and mountain ranges, I notice. Beds turned in a different direction, I don't.

I always have had to work up to a good cry. Sometimes, it takes me several hours and two six-packs to feel sorry enough for myself to start bawling. Not so with women, I learned. They can cry on cue, and they can cry about 'most anything. Special occasions, all the way down to Millard Fillmore's birthday, can make them cry. So can burned rolls, a broken tip on their eyebrow pencils, dead possums on the highway, soap operas, the fact that their husbands squeeze the toothpaste tube from the top rather than from the bottom, sunsets and sunrises, running out of gas, flat tires, dead batteries, the fact that they think their husband's secretaries are prettier than they are, an ounce of new weight, a cake that falls, watching *The Gift of the Magi* and *Miracle on 34th Street* at Christmastime, bottoms falling out of grocery bags, receiving a surprise bouquet of flowers, *not* receiving a surprise bouquet of flowers, getting their hair cut too short, spotting another woman at a party who is wearing a dress similar to theirs, Clark Gable's brush-off of Scarlett at the end of *Gone With the Wind*, their first wrinkle, a dying house plant, and being stopped for a traffic violation, just to name a few.

It is their ability to cry at the moment they are stopped for a traffic violation, as a matter of fact, that continues to keep the burden on men to pay most of the traffic fines in this country. Very few policemen are able to write out a ticket to a crying woman after they have stopped her. If a man cries after being stopped for a traffic violation, he risks being hauled in as some sort of pervert.

Only once have I ever seen a policeman strong enough to resist not giving a woman a ticket because she was crying.

Paula was behind the wheel of our 1966 Volkswagen Bug on her birthday as we drove along a state road. She was speeding. A county policeman pulled her over. The moment she saw the blue light of his patrol car begin to whirl around, she broke into tears.

The officer came to her side of the car, checked her driver's license, and began to write out a ticket.

"But officer," Paula managed to get out between sobs, "it's my birthday."

Sure enough. The officer checked her driver's license again and it was, indeed, her birthday. I knew what was coming next.

"Well, little lady," the average policeman would say, hoping to dry her tears, "we can't give you a ticket on your birthday, can we? I'll just give you a warning this time, and you try to slow down a little bit, O.K?"

Not this policeman. He motioned to his fellow officer waiting in the patrol car to join him. When the second officer arrived, the first said, "Guess what? Today is this little lady's birthday. What do you think we ought to do for her?"

"I don't know," said the second officer, "but I guess we ought to do something."

They looked at each other and were silent for a moment as the tension mounted. Suddenly they took a couple of steps back from our car and began to sing, "Happy Birthday to you.... Happy Birthday to you...."

When they were finished singing, the second officer went back to his car, and the first finished writing Paula her speeding ticket. I, meanwhile, was bent double in my seat, howling with laughter.

"You don't love me," she said as we drove away, a fresh batch of tears rolling down her cheeks.

What manner of men were these policemen? I thought to myself. How could they not crumple into putty as I always had when confronted by a crying woman? How could they possibly avoid the feeling of guilt?

Women cry because they realize that doing so will make you feel horribly guilty. It doesn't matter what they are crying about. If they are crying around a man, the man simply figures it's his fault, and he will go to any length, will apologize for anything, will promise everything, to make her stop crying. The best way to stop a woman from crying, however, is to take her in your arms put her head on your shoulder, rub the back of her head, and tell her you are sorry her cake fell, and that it probably was your fault in the first place, and that you, quite frankly, enjoy eating flat cakes.

Never do this while wearing a white shirt, however, because even good laundries have trouble removing mascara stains.

Before getting married, every man should take some sort of course to learn to deal with other complex matters, which will confront him as he begins to share his life and dwelling with a woman. Since, to my knowledge, there are no such courses, I offer here a brief rundown of some of the baffling ways of women, and what steps a man possibly may take to deal with them.

THE BATHROOM: Women spend most of their lives in the bathroom. They use the bathroom not only for toilet and bathing purposes, but also for a place to hang all sorts of undergarments for drying. Once married, a man will find his shower is no longer the safe and quiet retreat that it was before he was married.

After successfully crawling through fourteen pairs of wet panty hose drying on the shower curtain rod, a man will then find an amazing array of containers on top of the soap tray and on all sides of the tub. There will be nine different containers of shampoo, various hair conditioners, body oils, water softeners, bubble bath powder, odd sponges to be used for God-knows-what, a shower cap to match the shower curtain, facial soap, and personal items for feminine hygiene, some of which will look like they came out from under the hood of a Buick. Trying to bathe in the midst of all that hardware will make a man feel as though he is taking a shower in the bath items section of a K-Mart.

There will be other strange items a man will find on the bathroom dresser, where he keeps his razor, his toothbrush and toothpaste, shaving cream, and aftershave.

Suddenly, there will be added to those brushes and combs, electric hair curlers, blow dryers, hair spray, kleenex, a dozen or so bottles of makeup, various equipment for the maintenance of eyebrows and eyelashes, lip gloss and lipstick, bobby pins, barrettes, bands, nail polish and nail polish remover that smells like kerosene, cuticle removers and emery boards, powders and perfumes, and little boxes with flowers on them that hold little balls of colored soap that are purely decorative and are not to be used in any manner of emergency.

Towels are another matter. I need only one towel a week. I shower, I dry myself off, I hang the towel on the towel rack to dry, and when I'm ready for another shower, so is my towel.

Women use anywhere from three to five towels at a time, and they never use one again until it has been washed. Women need one towel to wrap around their hair after it has been shampooed. I don't know who teaches women how to wrap a towel around their heads after shampooing, but they are very adept at this procedure. The first time you see a woman with a towel wrapped around her head, you will think she has been converted to some sort of eastern faith and is wearing her prayer turban.

Women also use another towel to dry off their top parts, and then another to dry off their bottom parts, and after that, they still need one more towel to handle their faces. The towel issue becomes even more complex when a man discovers that not every towel he finds in his bathroom is for the purpose of drying off.

Women will inevitably go out and buy some large, fluffy towels with initials on them, and they will hang these all around the bathroom. If a man should happen to use one of these towels, a woman, having discovered this transgression, will make a lot of noise and accuse the man of having been raised with goats. These sorts of towels, a man eventually will come to learn, are placed in his bathroom for two reasons: one, for decorative purposes, like the little balls of soap, and two, for guests to use when they come over to dinner and have to go to the bathroom. It will seem quite odd to you that your wife will not allow her own husband to touch those towels, but will allow a perfect stranger who is visiting to dry off his hindparts with them, if he so desires.

Most women don't take showers. They take tub baths, and they take them for hours at the time, and they normally lock the bathroom door when they are in the tub. Once a woman is in a tub and has the bathroom door locked, it is basically impossible to communicate with her. They go deaf in a tub.

"Honey," you will say to the closed, locked bathroom door, "it's almost seven; are you about finished in there?"

"I can't hear you," she will inevitably respond. "I'm in the tub." I don't have any statistics to back this up, but I am almost certain that thousands of women must die each year in bathtubs, because they cannot hear the screams of their husbands and children and the sirens from the firetrucks, arriving to put out the fire in their houses.

Something else women do in the bathroom is shave their legs, and no matter how loudly a man protests, a woman always will use his razor to remove her unsightly leg hairs. She will always leave his razor on the side of the tub, making it necessary for him to search through the maze of bottles and tubes to locate his shaving tool, which, after three or four leg-shavings, will become a dull, yet lethal, weapon that will render his face a bloody mass of nicks and cuts.

I would suggest that, whenever possible, men and women should maintain separate bathrooms, and never, under any circumstances, should a man and a woman allow themselves to be caught in the same bathroom at the same time, lest they risk a certain quarrel and even, in some cases, murder-suicide that began when she ran a tub of steaming hot water that fogged up the mirror so he couldn't see to shave, and he cut off half his ear with the razor she had been using to shave her legs.

AIR CONDITIONING: Women are quite cold-natured, compared to men. Whenever the temperature dips into the eighties, they begin to shiver and complain, in a pitiful voice, "I'm cold." And no matter how much you might be perspiring, they fully expect you to turn down the air conditioning. If you subsequently pass out from the heat, so be it.

Women especially get cold at night. They will stack six layers of covers on the bed, even in July, and they will offer other subtle hints that you should cut down the air conditioning—like wearing woolen socks, your old high school letter jacket, gloves, and earmuffs to bed.

Women always complain about being cold in movie theaters, at ball games, in the car, at restaurants, and whenever they are bored and want to leave some such place. Bottom of the ninth, two out, the bases loaded, and you will hear, "When is this thing going to be over? I'm cold."

The best way to avoid the problem with air conditioning, and women getting cold at the worst possible time in the worst possible places, is to stay awake until they go to sleep and then cut the air conditioning back up, and never allow them to leave the house unless they are dressed like Nanook of the North.

COOKING: Paula was a tremendous cook, and I forever am indebted to her for the many marvelous dishes she set before me. No matter how good a cook a woman is, however, she eventually will fall to the temptation of experimenting in the kitchen. The kitchen is no place for experimentation, because strange things can happen.

Most men, I suppose, are fairly basic in what they like to eat. If I could have anything I wanted to eat, I would eat steak on Monday, pork chops on Tuesday, roast beef on Wednesday, country-fried steak on Thursday, barbecue sandwiches on Friday, another steak on Saturday, and fried chicken on Sunday. But that's too simple for most women.

"What are we having for dinner tonight?" I would ask my wife.

"Something different," she occasionally replied.

"Oh, my God," I would say to myself.

When a woman cooks "something different" for dinner, rest assured that, whatever the dish, it will be accompanied by some sort of strange sauce. I like gravy. I do not like sauces. The reason French people are so snooty is they eat too many sauces.

One night we had "something different," and it was called "Polynesian surprise." It was a surprise, all right. It was hot dogs with pineapple sauce poured on top.

Another time, we had some sort of Greek dish that was mostly rice with raisins in it. Uncle Ben was probably rolling over in his grave. Paula especially was eager to do weird things to chicken. Chickens basically have two purposes in this world—to lay eggs and to be fried. One night, Paula baked a perfectly good frying chicken and then put all sorts of strange vegetables on top, such as hearts of palm, bamboo shoots, and bean sprouts.

"What in the name of Colonel Sanders is this?" I asked.

"Hawaiian chicken," she answered.

"I should have guessed that," I said, "when I saw it was wearing a grass skirt."

The worst possible thing a woman can do in the kitchen, however, is to prepare liver. I hate liver. I refuse to eat it, no matter how it is prepared.

"You're going to like this liver," Paula would say. "I've cooked it with onions and green peppers."

"I don't care if you cooked it with Forty Mule Team Borax," I would reply. "I'm not about to eat any liver."

Women, however, inevitably will suggest that liver is good for you. I don't care if it grows hair and fights tooth decay, I still don't want any liver.

Women also will insist on putting celery in certain dishes. I hate celery, too. I also don't want to eat any pimento cheese sandwiches, stuffed grapes, bean casseroles, or anything with sweet pickles involved in any shape or form.

Something else I never wanted was any "ini" foods. "Ini" foods are those like zucchini and fettucini. One evening, Paula started experimenting with hot dogs again and served me a wienie with noodles all over it.

"I said I didn't want any more 'ini' foods," I commented as the meal was served.

"They're nothing but Italian hot dogs," she replied.
Oh, my God, I thought to myself. Wienieini.

DRINKING: Most women really do not like the taste of alcohol. That has led to the invention of all sorts of circus-like drinks that have so many other ingredients in them, there is no way to get any sort of alcohol taste whatsoever.

Some of these drinks are piña coladas, pink squirrels, strawberry, peach, or banana daiquiris, whiskey sours, apricot (believe it or not) sours, margueritas, vodka and cranberry juice, and anything with creme de menthe in it.

Paula, after her bout with the Jack Daniel's and Coke, would drink only those drinks mentioned above, or anything served with a little umbrella floating on top, or anything that you could drink and then keep the glass. One night we were at a Japanese restaurant that featured a fruit-like rum drink, served in a mug in the shape of a Sumo wrestler. Paula drank all the way to the wrestler's navel before she fell quite ill, and we had to leave the restaurant. She never drank anything out of a wrestler's belly again.

MONEY: I am certain there are many women who are very good at handling money, but I have yet to meet one. The fact that there are women who do not understand money is probably what has kept our country's free enterprise system going for more than two hundred years. Without women, there would be no after-Thanksgiving sales, no bargain days, no old-stove roundups, no once-in-a-lifetime offers on some device that rounds out cheese balls, and Gucci and Pucci would be just another couple of obscure Italian leathermakers.

I remain convinced that women were born to shop. They can spend hours searching for a bargain on Neet's Foot Oil; and if it happened to be on sale, they would buy a Shetland pony, figuring, in their twisted financial minds, that they actually have saved money by not waiting until Shetland ponies were marked up to their original price.

Women especially like to shop for antiques. I have seen them spend money on empty bottles, old bedpans ("They make wonderful flower pots."), old photographs of somebody else's grandparents, horse collars ("Won't this look nice hanging over the fireplace in the den?"), old wash tubs with the bottoms rusted out ("Isn't this the cutest thing?"), grappling hooks ("I don't know what I'm going to use these things for, but they were on sale for half-price.").

Women also enjoy shopping for trinkets. They will purchase, for instance, brass ducks. Why anybody would buy a brass duck is beyond me, but, thanks to women, the brass duck industry is flourishing. Women also will buy painted rocks and figurines of swans, lambs, and birds. They will buy wicker baskets, bowls of fake fruit to put on the dining room table, ashtrays in the shape of the state of Idaho, and anything made out of macramé, especially heads of owls.

Another valuable tip is never accompany a woman when she goes shopping for clothes. If you do, pack for a long trip. How a woman shops for clothes is, she goes to every store in town and tries on every garment and laments she can find absolutely nothing to fit her. Then she goes back to the first store and buys the very first thing she tried on.

Have you ever noticed there are no windows or clocks in most stores where they sell women's clothing? Merchandisers of women's clothing, like gambling casino operators, want to erase any sense of time or other distractions that might cause a potential customer to leave the premises without having first totally exhausted all funds, or at least having gone to the limit on whatever credit cards she might be carrying in her pocketbook.

When women shop for clothes, they basically are trying to alleviate their primal fear that there just might be a one-of-a-kind outfit out there somewhere, and if they don't find it first, their friend down the street might. It is this keen sense of competition that keeps a woman ever-vigilant in watching for new styles. Better to have died a small child than to be out-dressed at the next Tupperwear party.

There's something else that keeps women constantly in need of new clothing. Women's clothing doesn't hold up with age as well as men's clothing does. As a matter of fact, once an article of clothing has hung in her closet unworn for more than a ten-day period, that article of clothing becomes completely obsolete and couldn't be worn into a hardware store to pick up door hinges. Such aging garments are referred to as "that old thing" and could, perhaps, be recycled into warm clothing for our soldiers, if we are ever involved in another war.

Women have one basic rule when it comes to purchasing footwear: If the shoe fits, buy it. It used to bother me a great deal to know that there were people in impoverished countries going barefoot in the snow, when I would look into my wife's closet and see thirty pairs of shoes. I mentioned this concern to her.

"I agree, it's a shame," she said. "Why don't you ship off a few of my old shoes, and I'll go buy some new ones?"

Men's and women's feet are constructed basically the same, but women seem to need many more varieties of shoes than men. They have flats and high heels and round toes and square toes and pumps and sandals and shoes with straps and shoes with buckles. The worst thing that can happen to a man is for his wife to buy a pair of boots. Women normally buy shoes a couple of sizes smaller than their feet, because they never want to admit to themselves that their feet aren't dainty. This is no problem for a man—that is, until his wife can't get out of her new boots because they are much too small for her. It becomes necessary for the man, then, to pull and tug on the boots in an effort to get them off, and he will put forth this effort, unless he wants to sleep next to Dale Evans.

Women shouldn't buy hats, but they do. I have never seen a woman who improved her looks by wearing a hat. It is impossible to tell a woman that, however, so they buy outrageous hats.

Paula came home with a new hat once and tried it on for me.

"How do I look?" she asked.

Another rule: Never tell a woman she doesn't look good in some article of clothing she has just purchased.

"You look like a sort of cross between the Cisco Kid and Gabby Hayes," I replied, not aware of the aforementioned rule at the time.

When she stopped crying, I told Paula I was only kidding about her hat, that I really thought she looked very nice in it. She took the hat back anyway, and came home with another one that featured many feathers. It was all I could do not to say, "Well, Pocahontas, where'd you get the new hat?" but I knew better.

I finally did go out and apply for a credit card after college. Paula never really abused it, but there always was that nagging thought in the back of my mind that she would run across a bargain on a full-length mink coat and not be able to control herself, what with the magic of instant credit right at her fingertips.

Some men are not as lucky as I was when it comes to their wives using a credit card. Heed the legendary remark of tennis star Ilie Nastase, for instance, when his American Express card was stolen in New York. Reporters asked if he were trying to recoup the card. "No," said Nastase. "Whoever stole it is spending less than my wife was."

Money can become a source of much disagreement in a relationship between a man and a woman, especially if the man doesn't understand what his wife means when she begins talking about "our money" and "my money."

When she says "our money," she is talking about your money, the money you bring home in the form of a paycheck. "Our money" is used to pay all the bills and buy food and gasoline and deodorant spray, and other necessities of life.

"My money" is her money and hers exclusively. It is money she has either made from working her own job, or selling your golf clubs. Or, it could be money her grandmother gave her as a birthday present. "My money" can never be used on anything so mundane as living expenses. It is spent at her whim for such items as darling skirts and blouses. Never attempt, even in the most difficult of financial times, to locate "my money." Women rarely keep these funds in a bank, and often will resort to hiding it in the most amazing places.

The only man I ever knew who actually located and managed to get away with a woman's "my money" was my father. He had fallen on hard times and was spending a few days with his brother, my Uncle Frank, the lawyer. Uncle Frank was married to a rather strange woman, my Aunt Emily, a former fortune teller who had gone by the name of "Jilly Willie," and who had accumulated a small fortune in this profession. Aunt Emily did weird things with her "my money." For instance, she once brought home a small chihuahua dog.

"How much did you pay for that dog?" asked Uncle Frank.

"Five hundred dollars," said Aunt Emily.

"Five hundred dollars for a little dog like that?" asked Uncle Frank.

"Frank," answered his wife, "you know our daughter has asthma. The man who sold me this dog assured me that, if she held on to this kind of dog, it would cure her asthma."

Uncle Frank turned to visitors in the room and said, in an aside, "Every year, this country spends millions of dolluhs to ed-u-cate the heathen. Seems such a shame," he continued, peering over his glasses at Aunt Emily, "when we have such vast ignorance in our own midst."

Besides spending her money on such things as small

dogs, Aunt Emily also hid her money in strange places, such as under the frozen fish in her deep freezer and sewed into couch cushions.

My father soon felt the need to move on from his brother's home, but he did not have the capital for so much as a bus ticket. However, he did notice that in Aunt Emily's living room, there hung a sombrero over an opening that once had been a heating duct. My father slipped into the living room late one evening and removed the sombrero from the wall. Inside the opening behind it was sixteen hundred dollars in cash. Not only did he take the money and split, but when he boarded the bus for points unknown, he was wearing the sombrero.

Occasionally, we win one.

LOSING THINGS: I could go on and on about this, but I won't. The things women most often lose are their car keys. Their car keys normally will be found in the bottom of their pocketbooks, which are portable storage warehouses. Women often can hear their car keys jingling in the bottom of their pocketbooks, but they can't find them amongst all the other things they carry around in there, including canasta decks, yogurt, spare tires, and maybe even a length of garden hose. You never know.

What women lose most often, next to their car keys, are, in fact, their pocketbooks. How anybody could lose anything the size and weight of a bread truck, I don't know, but Paula spent half her waking hours searching for her pocketbook. She left it in any number of restaurants, a bus station or two, in church, and in the frozen food section of the grocery store.

Whenever she would begin to search for her pocket-book, that search would begin with her asking me, "Have you seen my pocketbook?"

What kind of question is that? I am a grown man, I would answer. I don't spend my time keeping up with the whereabouts of anybody's pocketbook.

Paula's pocketbook eventually would turn up, of course. Most of the time, the bananas and other assorted fruits she carried inside it would still be fresh.

GOING TO PUBLIC RESTROOMS: When women get away from home, it doesn't quell their desire to spend a lot of time in the bathroom. I am convinced that the female bladder shrinks to the size of a grape the moment a woman starts out on an automobile trip of any distance greater than three miles.

Whenever Paula and I traveled by car, we always added at least three hours to the normal driving time for restroom stops.

Five minutes after the trip began, I would notice her begin to squirm.

"I've got to stop and go to the bathroom," she would begin.

"Didn't you go before we left home?"

"Yes, but I've got to go again."

"Can't you hold it a little longer? I at least want to get outside the city limits before I have to stop."

"I can't hold it any longer."

Because of their anatomy, men can use the restroom just about any place; therefore, cleanliness of a facility normally doesn't enter into the decision-making process of where to relieve one's self.

A woman, however, will rarely go to the bathroom, except in an emergency situation, unless she is convinced it could be shown in *Better Homes and Gardens*. This, of course, makes even more stops necessary, since a wino would have to hold his breath in most service station restrooms.

"I couldn't go in there; we'll have to stop somewhere else," Paula would tell me upon returning from the women's restroom on our first stop.

"I thought you couldn't hold it."

"I can't, but that place was awful. I could have caught something."

There is no connection between filthy restrooms in service stations and any social diseases, but there are very few women who will believe that.

After our fourth stop, my wife would finally give in and go to the bathroom, no matter how rancid the facilities might be. Soon afterwards, however, her incredible shrinking bladder would be full again, and we could start the search for the proper place for her to empty it all over again.

I'm not certain what all is involved with going to the restroom in a public place for a woman, but have you noticed there is rarely a women's room in a theater or a stadium where there isn't always a line outside?

"It's that we have so much to take off first, and then we have to put it all back on again; that's why it takes a woman so much longer," it was once explained to me.

Quite frankly, I don't buy that. If the National Basketball Association were put in charge of women's public restrooms, it would install a twenty-four-second clock, and women would have no choice but to hurry, lest a women's room official make them give up possession of the stall in which they are sitting.

The most baffling thing about women and restrooms, however, is that, when eating out with other couples, women rarely go to the restroom alone.

"I'm going to the restroom," they will announce to the rest of the women at the table. "Anybody want to go with me?"

Women seem to be able to handle matters at home without any help, so why do they have to go to the restroom together when they are out in public?

"I think they go in there together to talk," a male friend of mine once offered as a possible explanation.

Maybe so, but why do they have to stay so long? What are they discussing, if they went in there to talk? Every detail of the rise and fall of the Third Reich? I can't recall ever going into a ladies room in a restaurant, but I would like to. Lord knows what I might find—boutiques, hair salons, maybe even slot machines and a fully equipped health spa. I don't care if you were wearing a deep-sea diving outfit and told your life story to your toiletmate, I don't see how women can spend that much time in a restroom. This phenomenon once prompted me to attempt to write a country song, entitled "When My Love Comes Back from the Ladies Room, Will I Be Too Old to Care?" The first verse went something like this:

My darling said she had to go,
It was half past eight o' clock.
She asked her friends if they'd go, too,
And they departed, a giggling flock.
At half past ten, they still weren't back
And I missed my one so fair.
And I wondered aloud, when my love
Comes back from the ladies room, will I
Be too old to care?

$*$ $*$ $*$

Paula and I moved to Atlanta after school. I was nearly twenty-two at the time, and I decided that I was an adult, and that it was time to do some adult things.

XI

Sing A Sad Song,
Faron Young

W E BOUGHT A small house in Atlanta and a lawnmower, and we furnished our den with a Naugahyde couch and chair and ottoman, and we furnished our living room with some delightful Spanish-style furniture that was on sale at the Big Red Furniture Barn. They also threw in a large portrait of a bullfighter, which we hung on the wall in the living room. There is a point in every man's life when he thinks that owning a portrait of a bullfighter makes him a connoisseur of fine art. Later, however, when he notices that portraits of bullfighters often are sold out of the backs of panel trucks on the side of the road, he realizes there is absolutely nothing tackier than a portrait of a bullfighter.

There is also a point in a man's life when he doesn't understand about living rooms and living room furniture.

Women are born, it would appear, with the knowledge that living rooms and living room furniture are to be seen and not sat upon.

"Why don't we go into the living room and sit on our new furniture and admire the portrait of the bullfighter?" I once suggested to Paula.

She recoiled with horror. "*Nobody* sits in the living room unless they have company," she said. "Everybody knows that."

I didn't know that.

"That's why we bought the Naugahyde couch and chair and ottoman for the den," she explained further.

I didn't know that, either.

"When we have some special company," Paula went on, "I'll take the plastic covers off the living room furniture and we'll sit out there."

"Special company," I also would learn, means the visitors must be no lower than a member of Congress or the Cabinet. I finally had to accept the fact that my hindparts likely would never touch anything but the cold reality of Naugahyde.

Becoming an adult for the first time offers the opportunity to learn all sorts of other things, too. I learned about life insurance salesmen, for instance. There were times when they waited in line outside my door in order to point out that I was going to die, and that I needed to leave my wife with a bundle of money. It had never occurred to me that I might actually die one day, and it also seemed a bit absurd to pour monthly payments into a deal that was designed to pay off only if I got run over by a truck.

Insurance salesmen, however, are very shrewd. They

realize that most men think buying life insurance—designed to make their wives filthy rich after they're gone—is a little bit ridiculous. But they also know how to put a man in a corner. They know that if a man refuses to buy life insurance, it's an indication to his wife that he doesn't care about her well-being after he's gone. The truth is that he doesn't mind providing for his wife after he's gone; he just doesn't relish the thought of some other son-of-a-gun helping her spend the jackpot.

What life insurance salesmen do is, they sit down with a man and his wife and say things like, "Buying life insurance is a way of saying you love somebody else more than you love yourself."

The wife is quite moved by such an eloquent statement and looks at her husband and wonders, does this turkey love me more than he loves himself?

Life insurance salesmen also say to the husband, "I know you will want to make certain that Hilda is well taken care of after you're gone."

The trap is then set. To suggest that after you're gone, Hilda can sell the bullfighter portrait and live off the proceeds, tells your wife there are limits to your affection and dedication for her, and a great deal of screaming and crying will ensue. What a man does to avoid this, then, is buy the life insurance policy and realize for the first time that he didn't just promise to love, honor, and obey until death did him part from his beloved; he also promised to keep her in silks and the latest appliances *after* his demise as well.

The loss of youthful innocence that accompanied my first steps into adulthood also revealed to me that some men spend a great deal of time plotting ways to get away from their wives. My male friends in college had been mostly single. At my job, however, most of my male friends were married. That same call of the wild that had plagued me for years, I discovered, also bedeviled other men.

"My problem," said a colleague, "is that five nights a week, I really enjoy being married. It's those other two that drive me crazy."

Atlanta was fast becoming a booming metropolis in the late sixties when Paula and I moved there. The singles bar phenomenon was also beginning, and in Atlanta, they couldn't build them fast enough. Underground Atlanta had the Bucket Shop and Ruby Red's, and on Peachtree Street there was the Chalet and Uncle Sam's; and the Brave-Falcon, so the rumors began to circulate down to me, was a teeming mass of fun and frolic nightly. Soon came Harrison's on Peachtree, where every night was Saturday night, especially Friday night, when the week-ending sun-down was celebrated with a Bacchanalia soon to become legend.

Some of my married friends could stand it no longer and romped into the revelry. Ah, the stories they told. Of incredible passionate adventures. Of bright lights and end-less delights. Of painted, willing darlings in white boots and hot pants.

It had happened to me again: I was forced to listen to the music from behind a closed door. The old frustrations came rushing back. Home was a warm place with pork chop dinners and the security of a constant, familiar partner. But my chains were choking me. My eyes were filling with greener pastures. Out there somewhere beckoned an evil temptress who promised unspeakable pleasures. And she was wearing white boots and hot pants.

*   *   *

I collapsed gradually. First, it was just a few beers with some of the men at the office after work. We would hit the Bucket Shop in Underground and tell a few lies and tales; then I would excuse myself and follow the path of the straight arrow home.

But the hours of such freedoms began to grow shorter and shorter. The clock constantly raced against me. The tinkling ice and the music and the laughter were all around me, and suddenly it was seven o'clock, and then it was eight, and one side of me said go, while the other begged to stay.

The telephone. The telephone was always a way to buy time. I had to call. Paula would be wondering why I wasn't home. I could call her and appease her. I could call and say I was okay, and I would be home soon, and that would satisfy her, and I could have that precious extra time for just one more, and maybe then just one more again.

The telephone is a flagrant liar. It makes promises it knows it can't keep. Nine o'clock would come and the dime would go into the slot and make that bell-like noise, and then there would be a ringing in my ear and Paula would answer.

"Where are you?" she would ask.

"At a bar," I would answer.

"Who are you with?"

"Some people from the office."

"What do you mean, 'people?' Are there girls, too?"

"Of course, there aren't any girls. Just some guys from the office."

"Do you know what time it is?"

"Of course, I know what time it is. What time is it?"

"After nine. Your dinner is cold."

"I ate a sandwich at the bar."

"You could have at least called."

"I tried, but the line was busy."

"I haven't been on the phone all evening."

"Maybe it was off the hook."

"It wasn't off the hook."

"Maybe it was out of order."

"Are you drunk?"

"No, I'm not drunk."

"You sound drunk."

"I think we have a bad connection or something."

"When are you coming home?"

"A couple of minutes."

I am certain that same conversation has taken place between millions of husbands and wives, especially the part where the husband says he will be home in a couple of minutes, which brings up a classic basis for misunderstanding between men and women. They don't tell time the same way.

To a man, a "couple of minutes" is merely a figure of speech. If he says he will be home in a couple of minutes, what he actually means is he figures the phone call has bought him at least another hour, and then maybe he can call again after that and purchase a little more precious time.

A woman's sense of time is quite literal, especially if she is waiting on a man to come home. When you say you will be leaving a bar in a couple of minutes, she thinks you mean you actually will be leaving the bar in a hundred and twenty seconds.

It's like pro football's two-minute warning. Very few women understand the two-minute warning.

"How much time is left in that silly football game?" they will ask.

"It's almost over," you answer. "They've just given the two-minute warning."

Women think that if it happens to be 4:15 at the time, the game will be over at 4:17, which isn't the case at all. The two-minute warning was conceived by men, for men, who realize the beauty of it. With two minutes to go before the end of each half, time is actually halted and everybody gets ready to go at it full force, with the ability to stop the clock again and again and again in order to milk every possible ounce of thrill and excitement from the activity in which they are engaged. The game can go on for another good half-hour after the two-minute warning.

It's the same for a man when he is out with his friends, drinking and having a good time. The call to his wife is his two-minute warning. In that final period, he has given himself a reprieve from the speeding clock. He will be able to savor his remaining time and possibly even avoid a desperate situation—his wife is waiting at home to kill him—by investing in that one telephone call.

I used to drink with a friend who took the analogy one step further. He came back after making the two-minute warning call to his wife, downed a couple of more, and then threw the most recently emptied can over the end of the other side of the bar.

"What are you doing?" asked the bartender.

"I don't have much time left," he said. "I'm throwing my beer can out of bounds to stop the clock."

My conscience wasn't taking any of this in an understanding manner. My conscience has always spoken to me with a voice that is a combination of my grandmother (Mama Willie) and Billy Graham. We had awful confrontations in those days, me and my conscience.

"What do you think you're doing?" it would ask me in that haughty, demanding tone it had developed back when I first yearned for forbidden fruits.

"Listen," I would say. "What do you expect me to do? I'm a young man in my prime. You want me simply to sit back and watch while the high times pass me by?"

"Nobody held a gun at your head and made you get married," my conscience would continue.

"What did I know when I was nineteen?" I would argue. "Anybody would have made the same mistake."

"You want to risk losing Paula?"

"I'm not sure."

"You mean you actually think you could live and be happy without her?"

"I don't know."

"You would miss her terribly."

"I know I would, but I would have my freedom then. Did you see that honey standing over at the bar tonight?"

"You're disgusting."

"You really think so?"

"I know so."

"I suppose you're right."

"Go home, sucker."

"I will," I would tell my conscience, "in a couple of minutes."

*   *   *

There was that song the truckers used to play at Steve Smith's back in Moreland. "Don't let me cross over love's cheatin' line," is how it went. It was a fine line, and men walked it like a tightrope—without a net—night after night in the bars. Listening to the instant replays of nightly excursions into the fastlane was an education in itself.

One of the veterans of the deceitful game explained how he was able to stay out all night and not get into serious trouble with his wife the next day.

"She's terribly afraid of my driving home when I'm drunk," he explained, "so about midnight I call her and pretend I'm totally out of my mind. She asks me where I am, and I make up something like I'm at a friend's apartment. She will always say, 'Don't you dare try to drive home. Stay right where you are and sleep it off.' After that, I've got the entire night."

Another explained he carried a container of talc around in his car. When he was going to be home late, he simply dusted his pants with the powder.

"I come in the door and my wife is screaming, 'Where have you been?' " he explained. "I say I've been hanging out at a bar, which is exactly what I've been doing. She sees the powder on my pants and says, 'No, you haven't. You've been out shooting pool again!' "

Knowing how to make up the proper excuse for staying

out all hours seemed to be the key for these married men who ran the singles bars successfully.

"No matter what," they lectured each other, "never admit you've been out chasing women."

Some examples of quick thinking in order to adhere to that rule were passed around. One man slipped into his house at five o'clock in the morning after a night out amongst the players. He quietly slipped off his shoes and was pulling his pants down his legs when his wife awakened. He quickly began to pull his pants back up again and said to his wife, "Sorry to wake you, honey, but I've got to be at the office early this morning." He put his shoes back on and out the door he went.

The classic example involved a man who came home just before dawn, after being warned by his wife that if he stayed out late one more time, she was taking the children and leaving him. As he walked into the house, his wife confronted him.

"Actually," he said to her, "I got home before midnight, but I didn't want to disturb you and the kids by coming into the house. So since it was such a nice, warm evening, I slept in the hammock in the back yard."

Great story, with one minor problem.

"I took that hammock down six weeks ago," the man's wife said.

"I don't care," he replied. "That's my story and I'm sticking to it."

There was also the matter of how to disguise the fact that they were married while in pursuit in a singles bar. There were certain rules men followed here, as well, I was told:

1. Never go into a singles bar wearing wing-tip shoes. Only married men wear wing-tip shoes.

2. Never drive a station wagon to a singles bar. Only married men with kids drive station wagons.

3. If you are lucky enough to get her phone number, make it clear you travel on company business most weekends. That way, she won't get suspicious when she notices that you call her only on weeknights.

4. Never admit your hobbies are refinishing old furniture or building model trains. Only married men have hobbies like those.

5. If you have to make your two-minute warning telephone call home, make sure she can't see you on the phone. You can tell when a man is on the telephone lying to his wife. He does a great deal more listening than talking.

6. Avoid dancing. Most married men are about two dance crazes behind.

7. Never talk about the great television show you saw last Saturday night. Only married men watch television on Saturday nights.

Getting caught, of course, was the ultimate risk. There were certain rules they followed in order to avoid that unhappy occurrence, too:

1. It is best to commit any illicit telephone numbers to memory, or keep them in a safe hiding place, such as behind the spare tire in your trunk. Even then, it is best to code the numbers. One suggestion for coding numbers was to reverse the first three digits and add one to each of the remaining four digits. It is also necessary, of course, to write down your code somewhere, in case you forget it.

2. Never say you are going bowling when you are really going out to a singles bar. No wife is that stupid.

3. Check your clothing for lipstick and eye shadow smudges. If you forget and your wife discovers such evidence, tell her you had to console one of your female clients who was crying about her upcoming lawsuit, and that's how the substances got on your shirt. If you're not a lawyer, call one.

4. Keep an onion handy at all times. On your way home from a night on the town, take a couple of bites. Your wife will never suspect you've been with another woman with your breath smelling like that.

5. Do not go out and buy a fancy new wardrobe for no reason at all. That's another dead giveaway to your wife that you are fishing in another pond.

6. Do not develop a sudden interest in getting a tan or slimming down your belly, for the same reason listed in Rule No. 5.

7. Do not change colognes. See Rule No. 5 and Rule No. 6.

8. If you talk in your sleep, pray that you mumble.

There was one other rule concerning fooling around: "If you play, you'll pay." Sooner or later, they all admitted, no matter how careful they were, they were going to get caught.

The worst case of getting caught I ever heard of involved a fellow who spent many evenings at Harrison's on Peachtree, one of the few early bars that has lingered on the Atlanta night life scene. It doesn't matter what his name was. I'll call him Phil.

The action was heavy at the front bar. Phil had joined a

young woman seated at a table near the piano. He was only moments away from closing the deal and leaving with the woman when the front door of Harrison's opened. In ran three small children. All were wearing their pajamas. The piano player stopped playing. The bartender stopped serving drinks. A hush fell over the entire place. It's not every day that three pajama-clad children walk into a singles bar.

Phil saw them, too. His face twisted in horror. First he thought of running. It was too late for that. Next he considered hiding behind one of the house plants. It was too late for that, too. Phil's three children ran directly to him at the table where he sat with the woman.

"Daddy!" they screamed in unison. "Mommy sent us in so you could kiss us good night."

Phil left the bar with his children. Somebody said he joined the church and quit drinking.

*   *   *

The Grim Reaper of divorce soon began to collect some of my wayward friends. One by one, they began to fall by the marital wayside. One man got caught with a pair of the wrong hot pants, and his wife kicked him out, changed the locks on his door, and then nailed his hide to the proverbial wall in divorce court.

"It could have been worse," he would say later. "If the judge could have given the death penalty in a divorce case, I think he would have."

Another's wife found his book where he kept the phone numbers and broke his code. She called nine numbers and got three "I-don't-know-what-you-are-talking-abouts," two "all-we-did-was-talks," and four full confessions. He had to take a room in a boarding house. It was all he could afford after the divorce.

I had never thought much about actually getting a divorce. All I knew were the stories from my acquaintances who were going through the experience. The judges had come down hard on all of them.

"Your lawyers couldn't do anything about that?" I asked them.

"A man goes into divorce court with two strikes against him," I was told.

Too bad my Uncle Frank wasn't still around. He probably could have helped them. One of my Uncle Frank's most famous cases, I recalled, involved a divorce. He was representing a man who claimed his wife had been unfaithful. Uncle Frank had to convince the jury that she was, in fact, the hussy her husband claimed her to be.

Uncle Frank struck with a subtle point:

"Ladies and gentlemen of the jury," he began, "I am not heah before you to recklessly attack the moral character of that young woe-man sittin' over theah, for to do so would brand me a man given to reckless use of gossip and hateful in-u-en-dooo. Howevah, I do have it on the highest authority that while this man, my client, was workin' in the hot fields, this woe-man heah, who wants to take his every penny, was seen dancin' on table tops at the Shorty's Truck Stop in Chattanooga, Tennessee, and further delightin' her audience by eatin' raw wienies." That was one case where the man didn't do so poorly.

Uncle Frank was gone, however, taken quickly by a heart attack. I'm not certain what ever happened to Jilly

Willie, his wife. Somebody said they had seen her several years after Frank's death, and, despite the fact that she was well into her seventies, she was wearing short shorts, driving a pink Cadillac convertible, and carrying two small poodles in her arms . . . thanks to Mutual of Omaha, and to Uncle Frank for keeping the premiums paid up.

*   *   *

Paula sensed my frustrations, I suppose. Of course, we never talked about them. My conscience tried to get me to be honest with her, but I held out.

"If you tell her what's going on inside you," my conscience said, "she probably will understand, and perhaps you can work all this out."

"Are you crazy?" I asked my conscience. "If I told her the truth, she would scream and cry."

"Honesty is always the best policy."

"Not if it makes somebody scream and cry."

"So you're going to say nothing?"

"You got it."

"You get more disgusting every day," said my conscience.

What I did, instead of telling the truth, was sulk a lot. Perhaps what I actually wanted was to get caught like my friends had, and then the decision would no longer be left up to me. Paula would kick me out and my freedom would be thrust upon me by someone else, and I would not have to bite the big bullet and go for the brass ring of regained singledom on my own.

"You gutless snake," said my conscience.

I was in a constant state of uncomfortable confusion. There I was wrestling with an unrelenting dilemma of whether or not to give in to the temptations of lustful pleasures, while Mama Willie and Billy Graham peered over my shoulders and churned my guilt.

*   *   *

Her name was Marla. She was sitting at the edge of the bar. We started talking. She liked me. I could tell. My heart pounded. My conscience nagged.

"Thou shalt not commit adultery," said Billy Graham in one ear.

"Remember how hot will be the fires of hell," said Mama Willie in my other ear. Strange, I suddenly thought I had caught the odor of burning eggshells and cantaloupe rinds.

Marla and I continued to talk. I looked at the clock. I raced onward.

"Why don't we go somewhere that's less crowded?" she said.

This can't be happening to me, I thought to myself. Would I actually go with her? Was this the moment I had been waiting for . . . and dreading? Was this what so many of my friends had given up loving wives and happy homes to achieve?

"It won't be worth it," said my conscience.

"Why don't you have a drink and stay out of this?" I said.

"I'm warning you. If you don't stop right here and go home right now, you're going to regret it."

"Let's have one more first," I said to Marla, stalling for time.

"Spineless jellyfish," said my conscience.

A few moments later, I found myself at the telephone again. I looked back at the bar. Marla smiled. Get thee behind me, Delilah.

I put a dime in the slot. The telephone made its bell-like sound. The phone was ringing. Paula answered it. Billy Graham threw his hands into the air in utter dismay. Mama Willie covered her ears so she couldn't hear.

I spoke into the phone.

"I'll be home in a couple of minutes," I said.

*   *   *

Midnight was a distant memory when I finally made it home. I found my clothes strewn all over the front yard. The door was locked. I banged on it until Paula finally opened it. We argued. She screamed and cried, and then ten years of my life just walked out the door. Actually, she didn't just get up and walk out the door. First she went and got my dog, and then she walked out the door.

My dog. He was a brown and white basset hound with droopy, sad eyes. His name was Plato. I had noticed, as the troubles had mounted in our relationship, that Paula had begun to transfer her affections to Plato. She even saved his life once.

Plato stopped eating all of a sudden, which was surprising, since eating was about all he did when he wasn't sleeping. We took the dog to the vet. The vet said Plato had a kidney disease and asked if we wanted him put to sleep. Paula wouldn't hear of it. Plato was costing me fifteen dollars a day in the animal hospital.

"He could linger for weeks," said the veterinarian. I

quickly multiplied the total again by four. Several, to me, has always been at least four.

A week passed: one hundred and five dollars.

"We've got to have Plato put to sleep," I said to Paula.

"Give him one more day," she begged me.

That night, Paula went to the animal hospital. She took Plato's favorite food with her. Fried chicken. White meat stripped from the bone. It had been no accident that whenever Paula fried chicken, I got the wing and thigh and Plato got the white meat stripped off the breast.

She sat on the floor of the animal hospital and held Plato's head in her lap. She put a small piece of chicken under his nose and urged him to try to eat it. He wouldn't. But after a couple of hours, Plato suddenly took a small sniff of the chicken, and then he took himself a small lick. A few moments later, he took a piece of the chicken into his mouth and swallowed it. Then he took another piece. Then another. Paula eventually fed him the entire plate of chicken, and the dog recovered. I fired off a nasty letter to the veterinarian for suggesting my dog should be put to sleep, when all he needed was to be hand-fed fried chicken to make him well.

As she was leaving me, Paula took hold of Plato's leash and began pulling him towards the door.

"You're not taking my dog," I said.

"Oh, yes I am," she continued. "I wouldn't leave this dog with somebody like you."

"He's my dog," I said.

"I'm the one who feeds him."

"He's my dog."

"He's going with me."

I tried to grab the leash out of her hands. Plato tried to bite me.

"If it means that much to you, then take the damn dog," I said.

She slammed the door behind her as they left.

"I told you so," said my conscience.

"I'll make do without her," I said. "Just watch me."

*   *   *

I moved into a small apartment with another fallen friend. Paula moved back to the house. We talked some. She even talked about trying to work things out. I hedged. I'll probably go back, I thought, but not before I see what it would be like to be on my own for awhile. This was the perfect opportunity, as I saw it. I could take my best shot at the single life, and if I didn't like it, I could go back home. It was easy to be smug. I had a net in case I fell.

I went out and bought myself a thin chain to wear around my neck.

"Creep," said my conscience. I didn't think it looked *that* bad.

I took to the singles bars night after night, but I was zero-for-every-attempt. Even the neck chain didn't help. I tried some new opening lines. I was smart enough never to use the "What's your sign?" standard, but "Is anybody sitting here?" and "Do you think Nixon will ever get us out of Vietnam?" certainly didn't produce very much either.

I remembered those girls in college who seemed so interested in me when I returned to school as a married man. Where were they now, for goodness sakes? What was the story here? Get married, and there are opportunities everywhere. Get loose, and they all disappear. Maybe I was wrong about those girls at college. Maybe all the girl in class wanted was to borrow a pen. Maybe all the girl at work wanted was the time. Maybe I wouldn't have been picked as the winning bachelor on "The Dating Game" anyway.

*   *   *

It was a Friday night at Harrison's. Women were everywhere. Short ones, tall ones, fat ones, skinny ones, ones in hot pants, ones in white boots, ones who would, ones who wouldn't, and ones you couldn't be certain about. I fired on everything in the place. I had to get lucky sooner or later. I talked to a girl wearing braces. I tried to drink her pretty. I couldn't. I talked to a girl wearing a bowling shirt. She had to leave for a league match.

The hour was late. The place had mostly cleared out. I was very close to going home with nothing more than the late edition of the newspaper. I spotted a woman seated on the bar stool at the corner of the bar. She would have been maybe a "six" three hours earlier. Add a point and a half anytime within thirty minutes of last call.

This was my chance. I went to the men's room first to make certain I was still as handsome as I thought I was. I walked back into the bar and sat down two stools from the woman at the corner. I tried to get a better look at her out of the corner of my eye. I decided the best I could do was give her one more point, tops. She was wearing a kimono. I had learned always to beware of a woman wearing a kimono. If a woman wears a kimono, it means she is not very proud of her figure, which means that up under that kimono somewhere is a camouflaged fat girl.

I didn't care. She was probably just as lonely as I was. So she would be a little overweight. We would have a few more drinks, and it wouldn't matter. We would go to her place, and maybe she would even make me breakfast in the morning. It beat waking up in that empty apartment.

I moved off my stool and sauntered to her side.

"I hate to see anybody drink alone," I said. I came up with that right off the top of my head.

Kimono looked me up and down and said, "Buzz off, creep."

When I arrived back at the apartment, it was quiet and dark. I missed my wife very much.

*   *   *

Men who leave their wives and rent apartments together usually wind up living like dogs. Green things grow on the dishes in the sink, because they are rarely washed. The refrigerator usually has plenty of beer, a frozen enchilada dinner or two, and a three-week-old carton of milk. The bathroom is cluttered with dirty towels and discarded underwear. The beds are never made up. The sheets would disgrace a tramp. Cigarette butts pile up in the only ashtray, and the carpet, if there is carpet, gets grimy. There are no curtains. Ants get into the week-old box of doughnuts that was left out on the kitchen table. Wrinkled clothes are scattered about the bedroom floors. There is mold at the bottom of the shower curtain. There is never any toilet paper. Empty beer cans, liquor bottles, and empty pizza boxes overflow out of the kitchen trash can.

I sat on the living room floor, watching the rented television, and surveyed this rancid scene, and I wondered what on earth had led me to believe I wanted to live this way.

Across town, I had a nice house and a pretty wife who loved me. I had traded that for a death wish of an apartment and fat girls in kimonos who called me names. I should have known better. Don't go looking for hamburger, somebody said once, when you've got steak at home. I traded my steak for bologna. What happened to all those plans of mine? What happened to that vow I had made to myself never to do what my father had done? As it turned out, I had made a lousy husband, too. At least he had an excuse. The war loused him up. I left, basically, because I thought there might be a party going on and I was missing it.

I was miserable. I hated the apartment. I hated singles bars. I hated myself. I was lonely. I was depressed. I was hungry. My underwear needed washing.

I decided to go back home and beg forgiveness. Just like that, I decided I had made a horrible mistake and I would go back home, never to stray again. I would never go back inside one of those wretched singles bars. I would put my ring back on my finger, and no arrow would ever fly straighter than me.

As I packed, I considered the best way to make my return to Paula. I could call her and say I was coming back, but, romantic that I was, I decided the moment of my return would be less dramatic if I informed her of my plans.

I wanted that moment to be splendid. I could see it in

my mind: I would drive up into our driveway. She would hear a car door slam, and she would look out the window of the living room and see it was me. She would notice the bags in my hand. The thrill in her would be almost too much to bear. He's home! He's home at last! She would fling open the front door and rush toward me in the yard. Her blond hair would be bouncing as she ran. She would jump into my waiting arms and cover me with kisses.

"How I have missed you!" she would exclaim breathlessly.

"And how I have missed you, my darling," I would reply.

We would go into the house and into our bedroom, and we would make passionate love until exhaustion forced us into a peaceful sleep together. In the morning, we would make love again and then talk for hours in our bed, planning each step in our future. We would build our bridge over our troubled waters, as Simon and Garfunkel were singing in those days, with sacred promises.

I couldn't pack my bags fast enough. I left the apartment and aimed myself home. Halfway there, a few feelings of anxiety began to creep into my consciousness. What if Paula weren't home when I arrived? Of course, she would be at home. Where else would she have to go on a Saturday evening? What if she didn't want me anymore? Ridiculous, I thought. We've been in love since we were fourteen. She had been sitting there pining for me for nearly a month; of course, she would want me back.

I was less than a mile away now. My heart pounded. My stomach churned. I took off my neck chain and threw it out of the window of my car.

I began to picture the scenario of my arrival again

Maybe after we had made love, Paula would fix me something to eat. Pork chops, maybe, with creamed potatoes. And when I awakened in the morning, I likely would discover that she had arisen during the night and washed my clothes. Think of it. Clean underwear. It would be wonderful to be back home.

There was the house. There was a light on in the living room. Her car was parked out front. I had been foolish to think she might not be there. She would be running out of the house and into my arms, and I would be smothering her face with my lips in only a matter of seconds!

I pulled into the driveway and turned off the engine. I stepped out of the car and slammed the door. I looked for her face in the window. I didn't see it. Maybe she was in the bedroom or the kitchen, I thought, and hadn't heard the slamming of the door. I opened it and slammed it again. Still, she didn't come out.

I slammed the door a third time. Nothing. Maybe she was sleeping. Maybe she had the television turned up. I was disappointed that there apparently was not going to be the passionate first-meeting in the front yard, but we could greet each other just as affectionately as I stepped through the door into the living room.

I thought about ringing the door first. But why should I ring the doorbell? This was my house. I opened the door and stepped through it. I waited anxiously for Paula's appearance. There was no sound whatsoever in the house. I dropped my bags. I walked into the kitchen. She wasn't there, either.

Finally, I called out to her. The door to our bedroom opened. She stepped into the hallway. We were twenty feet away from each other. Our eyes met. She didn't rush to greet me. She just stood there, staring at me.

"What are you doing here?" she asked.

"I've come home," I said.

"For what?"

"For good."

"You've come back here to live?"

"Forever."

"Why didn't you call first?"

"I wanted to surprise you."

"You've surprised me."

"Are you happy to see me?"

"Well. . . ."

"You're not happy to see me?"

"I'm happy to see you, but it's a little bit of a shock. You could have called first."

"I should have called first."

"Are you sure you know what you're doing?"

"Positive."

I walked closer to her. This wasn't the way it was supposed to have been at all. Maybe she was still in shock. Seeing her prayers answered right out of the blue probably was so overwhelming that she was having a difficult time absorbing the joyous reality of the situation.

I put my arms around her and I kissed her. She likely would have kissed me back a bit more emphatically, had she not been in shock. I likely would have taken her directly to bed, had her hair not been up in curlers.

*   *   *

It lasted five months. I stayed out of the bars. I took to

working in the yard in the afternoons. I even cooked dinner for Paula occasionally.

She was having to work late a lot, and she and her girlfriend often stopped on the way home to have a few drinks, which was fine by me. A woman needs a little time to be off with her friends, too.

She usually called me at home when she was going to work late or was going out for a drink. One evening, she didn't. Seven o'clock came, so I went to the kitchen and whipped up some dinner. She would be home soon, and she would be too tired to cook. Lucky for her, she had someone as caring as me to relieve some of the domestic burden at times like these. That's the secret to being happily married, I told myself, sharing. I should have learned that years before, watching my grandparents. Mama Willie cooked the chicken. Daddy Bun wrung its neck and plucked out its feathers. Sharing.

Eight o'clock. I'd cooked spaghetti. Nothing to spaghetti. Some ground beef, some onions, tomatoes, and a little oregano. I put the spaghetti into the refrigerator. When Paula got home, I could warm it up again. She worked hard, too. She deserved unwinding a little after work. I'd done it. And when she came home, she would be hungry, and I would have her something to eat. Sharing.

Nine o'clock. No call. At least she could call. I took out a bottle of Jack Daniel's and poured it over ice and covered that with Coke. I went into the den and put on my Faron Young albums. I listened to "Hello Walls" and "She Thinks I Still Care."

Ten. I turned the records over again.

Hello, walls. How'd things
Go for you tooo-day?
Don't you miss her,
Since our darlin' went
Awaaaay...."

There were lights in the driveway.

Just because I asked a
Friend aboooout her.
Just because I spoke
Her name somewheeeere.
Just because I dialed
Her number by mistake
Toooodaaay,
Sheeeee thinks I
Still caaaaare.

I didn't get off my seat on the couch when Paula walked in. It was nearly eleven o'clock. The Jack Daniel's bottle was nearly empty. She could have at least called.

"You could have at least called," I said.

"I tried," she said. "But the line was busy."

"The phone hasn't rung all night."

"Maybe it was out of order."

"Where have you been?"

"With friends."

"What were you doing?"

"We were just having a few drinks. I didn't realize it was as late as it is."

"You hungry?"

"I already ate."

"I cooked spaghetti."

"We'll eat it tomorrow."

"I love you."

"I love you, too. I'm going to bed."

"I'm going to sit up a little longer."

After Paula went to bed, I thought about calling my mother. But it was late. She would have already been in bed for a couple of hours. I poured out the last of the Jack Daniel's and turned Faron Young over again.

Hello, ceiling,
Think I'll stare at you for awhile....

*   *   *

She left me a long letter. I had trouble reading it, because she still wrote in that strange, backwards, left-handed manner. I came home and found the letter lying on our bed.

She said she couldn't live with me any longer. She said so much had happened. She said I had hurt her, and she was having a lot of trouble forgiving me. She said she didn't feel as if she could be a good wife to me anymore. She said maybe later she could, but that she needed some time to think about it.

Plato was gone. So were most of her clothes. She didn't put in the letter where she was going. They never do. I tried to call her at work the next day, but she wouldn't take my calls. I thought of going to her office and making some sort of scene. Then I decided against that. I likely would just make a fool of myself. I called my mother.

"She'll come back, son."

"You think so?"

"She'll come back."

I called Paula's mother.

"She just needs some time."

"Do you think she'll come back?"

"I don't know. You've got to give her some time."

Time. How much time? A week? A month? A year? What was I supposed to do in the interim? At least in that God-awful apartment, there had been no reminders of her. Here, in our house, she was everywhere. Our wedding picture sat on the dresser. She left behind a couple of nightgowns. They looked like her. The pillow next to me in our bed still smelled like her hair.

She finally agreed to talk to me one afternoon when I called her at work. She had taken an apartment, she said. She wouldn't tell me where.

"I don't want you coming there," she said. "I want you to leave me alone."

"Can't we just talk?" I asked, I pleaded.

"We don't have anything to talk about," she said.

The first week was awful. The second was worse. Then it had been a month. I tried to call the minister who married us. Maybe he could get in touch with her and tell her how important it was that she come back to me. Maybe he could quote her some scripture.

He agreed to write a letter, but he said he didn't know how much good it would do, especially with the fact he was no longer a minister. He had quit preaching and opened a used car lot.

I tried to find my father. Maybe he could help me when nobody else could. He'd been through this. He had lost his wife and his son, and he would know what this felt like. I had never gone to him for advice before. I hadn't spent six weeks with him in the past seventeen years. He had wandered from job to job, town to town. He had remarried twice. Neither had worked out. I knew why. He couldn't get Christine, my mother, out of his mind. He could tell me what to do, what not to do. A man needs his father at a time like this, I said to myself.

I called the Dempsey Hotel in Macon.

"Haven't seen him in three months," said the bellman.

I tried some of his relatives. They didn't know where he was, either.

Another month passed. I wrote Paula long letters and sent them to her office. She never answered them. The house was in a shambles. The sheets were dirty, the ashtrays were filled, dirty underwear was strewn all over the bathroom floor, the garbage can in the kitchen was overflowing.

Where was my father? Probably drunk somewhere. The one time I need him worse than I have ever needed him before, and he has vanished from the face of the earth.

My aunt, my father's older sister, called late one night. She had located my father. He was in a hospital in Claxton, Georgia, a few miles west of Savannah.

"He's dying," said my aunt.

XII

'He Don't Deserve No More Hell'

JOHN WESLEY GRIZZARD, still stout and strong in his seventies, pulled the cup of coffee to his mouth, took a sip, and then followed that with a long drag off the Camel cigarette he held in his other hand. His fingers were yellowed from the miles of nicotine-laden smoke that had passed over them. His younger brother and business partner, Walt, had died from cancer. John Wesley had closed down Grizzard Motors after that and moved out to the country.

"I still mess with a few ol' cahs now and then," he said, "but I don't take it as serious as I used to."

It was almost four o'clock in the morning. We sat in an all-night truck stop on some God-forsaken highway near Claxton in southeast Georgia. My father had been in the area for more than six months, we learned. He had married an older woman, and she had taken him in and fed him and bought him some new clothes. And for a time, he had been off the booze and had even gone to church suppers and had done a little singing in the choir.

But that didn't last. It never did.

He had suffered a mild stroke a couple of years earlier, but he had recovered. Then, walking through the streets of Claxton, a few miles from his third wife's home in Pembroke, he had collapsed again. Somebody called an ambulance and he was taken to the Claxton hospital. Another stroke, was the diagnosis. This time, it was much worse than the previous one.

All they found on him at the hospital was a watch and a ring and an empty wallet. That, and a letter inside his coat pocket. The letter was from me. I had written it to him two years earlier. They called his wife from the hospital and told her of his condition. She said there was nothing she could do, that she hadn't seen him in weeks, that he was bad to drink, and that she had no further intentions of being involved with him. She had agreed only to inform a member of his family, my aunt, who lived in Atlanta.

"You had better go see about your daddy," my aunt had said.

John Wesley came on the line. "I'll go with you, son."

We left Atlanta at eleven. The drive, over dark, two-lane roads, took us more than four hours. We talked about my father on the way to the hospital.

"I don't know what happened to your daddy," said John Wesley. "I guess a man sees all that death and dying in two wars, and he never gets over it."

I really didn't have a reply. We continued to cut our way through the heat and dark of the August night.

John Wesley lit another Camel and said, "Your daddy loves you. You know that, don't you, son?"

I fiddled with the radio. I got a late baseball game from the west coast. The Cardinals and the Giants on KMOX out of St. Louis.

"I know he loves me," I said to my uncle. I think I know he loves me, I said to myself.

I thought about Paula. Would she care that my father was dying? Of course, she would care, but would she care enough to help me through this? Maybe this would get us back together, I thought. Maybe she will realize how much I need her, with my father dying, and maybe she will come back and feel sorry for me. Perhaps one door is closing and another is opening. I would lose my father, but I might get my wife back. I realized, given a chance, that I would make that swap without a second thought. It made me feel only slightly guilty.

We walked into his darkened hospital room at three in the morning. He was unconscious. The night nurse said we could stay only a couple of minutes. He had bruises.

"We think that's from where he fell when he had the attack," said the nurse.

I didn't know what to do.

"Think we ought to pray?" I asked my uncle.

"Go ahead if you want to, son," he said. "But I've never been much of a prayin' man, myself."

I wanted to pray, but I couldn't think of what to say. I rubbed my father's sweating forehead a couple of times, and then the night nurse said it was time to leave.

We found the all-night truck stop. Outside, the moths and beetles swarmed around the lights. Inside, a woman sat in a booth with a man who was barefoot and drunk. She was trying to force coffee down him. The waitress behind the counter was missing her two front teeth. On the wall behind the counter, with the displays of handkerchiefs, combs, cigarette lighters, and cans of Prince Albert tobacco, was a wooden plaque that pictured the cartoon figure of a pregnant woman, with the words, "I should have danced all night."

John Wesley smoked and drank his coffee without speaking. I ordered eggs and toast. The eggs were runny. The toast was hard. A small, green bug flew into John Wesley's coffee and died there. He dipped his finger into the cup and removed the bug and continued drinking his coffee.

My thoughts went back to when I was a small boy and my mother was in the hospital, and they thought she was dying. My father had said she was going to go away. He had said she was going to heaven. He had said that later we would go there and be with her.

"What was your mother like?" I asked John Wesley. "She died before I was born."

"Fine little woman," he answered. "She loved your daddy."

"Do you believe that when you die, you go to heaven and see your parents again?" I went on.

"Can't say I do," he answered.

My father had looked so pitiful, so helpless, in that hospital bed. Maybe the last peace he had known came from the gentleness of his mother, Miss Genie. I wanted to think that if he did die, then at least he would be with his mother again. Maybe she could ease the demons that raged in him.

"For his sake, I hope it's true," I said.

"Whose sake?" he asked.

"Daddy's," I said. "I hope he goes to heaven and I hope he sees his mother again."

"Yeah," said John Wesley. "He don't deserve no more hell."

We sat side by side on the counter at the truck stop until dawn. The drunk passed out on the table and the woman left him there. The waitress made a batch of fresh coffee, and John Wesley took a cup to go.

"Let's go see about your daddy," he said. "I'm tired of drinking coffee with bugs in it."

He lingered on for three more days. John Wesley and I shared a room in the only motel in town. The doctors said there was no hope. The stroke had left him without speech and without the use of his right arm and right leg. Even if he did survive, he would be an invalid.

"Better off dead," said John Wesley. I agreed with him.

After the third day, my uncle was restless.

"Nothing more we can do for him here," he said. We decided to drive back to Atlanta. I would return as soon as possible, or the moment there was a drastic change for the worse. I left my telephone number with the hospital.

When I arrived back home, I called my mother.

"I think he's going to die," I said to her.

"He's lived a hard life," she said. "Maybe he would be better off."

"That's what Uncle John Wesley said. I guess you're right."

"Don't worry about him. There's nothing you can do."

"I know. I just wish I could have talked to him one more time. Maybe I could have straightened him out."

"Nobody could," said my mother. "I gave up a long time ago."

"First Paula, and now him," I said.

"You've got your whole life ahead of you, son. You'll get over all this."

"Do you want to see him before he dies?" I asked my mother. "You can ride down with me."

"I don't think I'd better," she answered.

I understood.

"But I want you to think back and remember something," she went on. "I never tried to turn you away from your daddy. I never said one bad word about him in front of you, did I?"

She hadn't.

"He was a good man. He just got lost. Don't ever think anything bad about him. He did what he had to do. Just learn from his mistakes."

Two days later, my telephone at my bedside rang. It was 4:30 in the morning. The night nurse was calling.

"You'd better come," she said.

"It's bad?" I asked her.

"It's real bad," she answered. "He could go at any time."

I drove hard. I walked into the hospital room less than four hours later. He was blue. He was literally blue.

"He has pneumonia," said the nurse. "He can barely breathe."

I held his hand. He was dead within ten minutes after I

arrived. A doctor came in, checked his pulse, and declared him dead. A nurse pulled a sheet over his face. I wondered why they always pull a sheet over somebody's face when they die.

I asked to be alone with my father. I cried. I prayed there was a heaven and that he was in it.

I called my mother.

"He died fifteen minutes ago," I said.

"Was he in any pain?" she asked.

"No," I said, "he never even knew I was in the room."

My mother said she would come to the funeral.

I called Paula at work. I came right to the point.

"I need you," I said. "I need you to help me through this."

"I'll be at the house when you get back," was her instant reply.

*   *   *

We put him next to his mother in the little cemetery in front of the home church, Zoar Methodist, outside Snellville in Gwinnett County. I found a bugler to play "Taps." I got an honor guard from the local VFW chapter. They wore their caps and they stood at attention throughout the service. They furnished a flag. Two of the men folded it off his casket and handed it to me. Paula, who was sitting next to me at the grave, squeezed my hand when they handed me the flag. My father was fifty-eight.

Paula had met me at our house as she said she would do, and she had cleaned it and she had cooked me something to eat. She stayed the night before the funeral, too, and she went home with me after the funeral. I was exhausted from the ordeal I had just been through. We went to bed early. I fell asleep in her arms. In the morning, we would talk, and then in the afternoon, I would go with her to her apartment and we would get her things and bring them back, and we would start our lives together for the third time.

She was gone when I woke up. There was no note. At the foot of the bed was a laundry basket. She had arisen early. She had washed and folded my underwear, and then she had left.

She never came back. I continued to plead with her over the months, but she wouldn't listen. What could it be? I was changed. I had no intentions whatsoever of treating her as I had before. Had I been all that bad of a husband? Hadn't we shared nearly ten years of our lives together? What could be holding her back?

Christmas. I drove home to Moreland on Christmas Eve to spend the night with my mother and H.B. I had called Paula in the afternoon. I had told her I had a present for her. She said she would be spending the night at Miss Inez's in Moreland. I had bought her a coat, a beautiful coat, the kind of coat her mother had told me she wanted for Christmas, when I had called to ask her advice. I was desperate. If I went out and bought her an expensive coat, I reasoned, maybe she would finally realize how much I cared for her. Christmas had always been special between us. This was my last-ditch effort.

I called Paula from my mother's house. I asked to come over and bring her present.

"I don't have you very much," she said. "I was short on money."

I said I didn't care. I meant it.

We sat in her den, Paula and me and her mother and father. It was awkward. Paula's parents, despite our troubles, always had treated me with kindness. They had listened to my promises, too. A few too many Jack Daniel's, and I would call and talk to one of them, and I would end up crying over the phone, and I would hate myself the next morning. But they seemed to understand.

I gave Paula the coat. She gave me a cigarette lighter. I asked if we could go for a ride. I dreaded spending Christmas Eve without her. Maybe I could convince her we could spend the night together. We weren't divorced. Our parents would understand.

We drove around Moreland, around the church where we were married, around the school where we first met. We parked alongside the baseball field where she had watched me play.

I took her hand. I spoke quietly and deliberately.

"We can't let this get away from us," I said. "We've been together too long. We will never find anybody else to love as much as we love each other."

She listened without speaking. I droned on and on, searching for the right phrase, the right word to convince her we belonged together. I made every promise that came to my mind.

"I was wrong," I said, "but I didn't know any better. I had to find out there was nothing to life without you. And there isn't. I know you know that. You've been alone too. . . ."

I paused in mid-sentence. It came to me that fast. All these months, I had thought she was simply afraid that I might look elsewhere for affection again. I thought she was trying to test me, to see whether or not I really had changed, to see if I really did love her and want her as much as I said I did. But that wasn't it at all. What a fool I was. What an idiot.

"What's his name?" I asked. She told me. I asked her if she loved him. She said she wasn't sure. She said he wanted to marry her. I suddenly had trouble breathing. I asked her when it had happened. She said they worked together. After I had left her, she went out with him a few times. She had been so confused, so lonely. I asked why she had allowed me to stay when I came back. She said she didn't know why. I asked her if she continued to see him after I came back. She said occasionally. I asked her about the night I cooked the spaghetti and sat there drinking Jack Daniel's and listening to Faron Young and she didn't come home until eleven o'clock. She said all they had done was talk. I asked her if he was the reason she had moved out. She said yes. I asked her if I could spend the night with her. She said no.

Late Christmas Eve night, my mother walked out of her bedroom and came into the living room, where I sat on the couch, staring at *Miracle on 34th Street*.

"Did you talk to Paula?"

"We talked."

"Is there anything I can do?"

"No."

"Do you think you will work things out?"

"I don't think so."

"Are you sure there is nothing I can do?"

"Put your arms around me," I said. I cried on her shoulder. "I should have treated her better," I sobbed.

"We never know those things until it's too late," she said. "I'll squeeze you some orange juice. You'll feel a lot better."

*   *   *

We divorced. Paula got Plato. I got my Naugahyde couch and chair and ottoman. She got the stereo and all my records. I missed her. I missed the dog. I missed Faron Young.

She married soon afterwards. She moved out of town. She had a baby.

XIII

A Bad Case of
Black Cord Fever

IBOUGHT SOME BEER and I bought some cheese, and I put them into my refrigerator. I worked nights. When I got back to my apartment, I enjoyed having a few beers and eating some cheese.

I had two roommates. Wild men, the both of them. They ran hard. I came home after work and their doors were closed. I could hear laughing sounds inside their rooms. They each had a woman in their bedroom, and all I had was beer and cheese.

An hour later, the doors opened and two women walked out. Hookers. You can tell a hooker.

"Your friends are passed out," one said to me. "How 'bout taking us back downtown."

"What do I look like?" I asked. "A Yellow cab?"

"You got any more beer?" they asked me.

"In the refrigerator," I said.

They each got themselves a beer and a slice of cheese. There I sat, a grown man from a fine Methodist family, educated in a large Southern university, drinking beer and eating cheese with two hookers at two o'clock in the morning. I got up and tried to awaken my roommates. They were both dead men. While I was gone, the two hookers drank the rest of my beer and ate the rest of my cheese.

"Take us back downtown," they said.

"I've been working all night," I said.

They offered a trade-out.

No way.

"We got to get back downtown," they continued to plead. "We don't get back pretty soon, our old man is going to beat hell out of us."

Old man?

"Our pimp. Don't you know nothing?"

"He beats you?"

"We get an hour for each trick. It's been longer than that already," said one of the hookers.

I studied them. They were both in their early twenties, I figured. They wore the complete outfit: white boots, hot pants, see-through blouses.

"How much did those two turkeys in there pay you?" I asked them.

One was much prettier than the other, in a hustling-sailors-on-the-corner-in-front-of-the-bus-station sort of way.

"I get fifty," said the prettier one. "She don't get but thirty-five."

The less attractive of the two looked somewhat embarrassed

when her partner mentioned the discrepancy in their rates. Fifty and thirty-five, I thought to myself. Where were you two in 1964?

"Your pimp really beats you?"

"He put me in the hospital once. I ain't going to mess with him again," said fifty.

"Why don't you call a cab?" I asked.

"Ain't enough time for that," answered thirty-five. "You got to take us back downtown."

They crawled into the seat next to me. What could I do? I didn't want it on my conscience that I had been a party to two hookers being brutally beaten by their pimp.

I drove to town. They asked me to let them out in front of the Sans Souci night club. All the way, I had been thinking of Sally Gladstone. I wondered if she had turned out like this. I owed Sally one, I thought. This was the least I could have done.

The two hookers got out of my car. I looked around for the pimp.

"Be careful," I said to them. "Tell your old man the two guys you were with passed out and you had to hitchhike back downtown, and that's why you were so late."

I marvelled at my own sensitive nature. I had befriended two beer-guzzling, cheese-eating hookers in the middle of the night.

"Don't sweat it, sucker," said fifty. I watched as they hit on two conventioneers and disappeared with them into the nightclub.

*   *   *

The first thing a newly divorced man does is put posters up on the walls of his apartment. He secretly wanted to have posters on his walls when he was married, but his wife insisted on prints of fruit baskets and little girls picking flowers, instead. Putting posters on his wall is a man's way of expressing the independence he has suddenly gained, regardless of whether he wanted it or not.

I found a poster for my kitchen that pictured a large sheep dog with hair all over its face. The caption read, "My life is just one headwind after another." A newly divorced man naturally feels sorry for himself, and he can look at a poster like that and encourage such self-pity.

I had another poster in my bedroom of a girl standing on a tennis court wearing a tennis dress. Her back was to the camera and she had pulled up her dress slightly, in order to scratch her rear. She was wearing no underpants in the picture. I'm not certain exactly why that poster appealed to me, but it did. In my bathroom, I had a poster that showed giant waves breaking in the ocean. The caption read, "Life Is a Daring Adventure or Nothing at All." Helen Keller said that. Each morning that I went into my bathroom with a terrible hangover, I looked at that poster, and it made me feel better about whatever daring adventure the night before had left me in my current condition.

A man will further decorate his apartment in "Early Divorce," which basically is whatever furniture, if any, he received in the property settlement, with a few other selected items that were on sale at K-Mart. I had my Naugahyde couch, chair, and ottoman. Naugahyde furniture is fine, as long as you aren't sweating. If you are sweating, you tend to stick to Naugahyde. I also had my green reclining chair that had a split in the seat, and a lamp that featured the face of a pelican. I picked up a second-hand bed cheap, and then I went to K-Mart for bedclothes, including an extra pair of sheets and pillowcases, which I never got around to putting on my bed, because it was too much trouble to wash the ones already on it.

I didn't buy any trinkets whatsoever. I didn't want any brass ducks, any figurines of lambs, or any owl heads made out of macramé. I vowed never to waste money on such items again. I didn't buy any little decorative soap balls, either, and I could go a week on one towel. And if there isn't a woman sharing your living quarters, there is absolutely no reason to purchase toilet bowl deodorizers, tablecloths, placemats, Brillo pads, oven cleaner, skin lotion, or Kleenex. I have never found any reason to buy Kleenex. I don't wear makeup that needs wiping off, and if I have to sneeze, I use either a handkerchief, my hands, or toilet paper.

A newly divorced man also saves a great deal of money on food. You fill your refrigerator with frozen dinners, luncheon meat, individual slices of American cheese, a jar of mayonnaise, and beer. The only other food you need is a couple of cans of pork and beans, a loaf of bread (half of which will be covered with mold after a week or so), a carton of milk that will eventually sour, and several cans of chicken noodle soup. I ate so much chicken noodle soup the first six months I was divorced, I developed this strange urge to go outside and peck corn.

Examples of foodstuffs a newly divorced man will *not* have to fool with anymore include radishes, lettuce, and celery; rump roasts, lamb chops, and any other meats that can't be thrown into a pan and fried; and anything that is involved in making a congealed salad. Women insist upon making congealed salads, which nobody really enjoys eating. Women like to make congealed salads because they are colorful and can be made to match the tablecloth. Congealed salads, in reality, are nothing more than glorified gobs of Jello, and dogs won't eat them, so neither will I.

What else a newly divorced man will do is go out and buy himself a new wardrobe. I bought myself five pairs of double-knit trousers and several new shirts, all of which featured interesting patterns, such as palm trees, Indianapolis-type racing vehicles, and large green frogs playing flutes. I also bought a double-knit paisley sport coat, a leather jacket (which was the rage of the day), and a pair of white shoes. I looked like I had just stepped off the cover of the J.C. Penney spring catalogue.

For the first time in my life, I had total freedom to do what I pleased. I had no parents to answer to, no girlfriend demanding my weekend allegiance, no wife sitting at home awaiting my telephone calls. If I wanted to run singles bars, I could run singles bars. If I wanted to stay out all night, I could stay out all night. If I wanted to throw my underwear on the floor, I could throw my underwear on the floor, and there was nobody to complain about it. And I could squeeze a tube of toothpaste at any point I desired.

Those are the primary advantages of being free as the eagle flies and freshly divorced. The disadvantages are that your parents incorrectly think you are old enough to take care of yourself; you never have anything to do on the weekends; nobody cares if you call them or not; singles bars can be terribly depressing; if you stay out all night, you feel miserable all the next day; you live in a certain degree of squalor; and if you don't squeeze the toothpaste from the bottom, the top of the tube becomes flat, and it is almost impossible to get toothpaste still left in the bottom of the tube out through the flat part of the top and onto your toothbrush.

There is something else about the sudden freedom gained from divorce. You aren't exactly certain what to do with it. Sharing a life with someone else brings with it a certain order to things. You know what you can do and what you can't do, and everything has its time and place.

Not so for the man in the early stages of divorce. You eat and sleep when you can, and work when you have to. You can't find socks that match. You need to change the beneficiary of your life insurance, but you'll try not to die this week and set up an appointment with your agent the next. You forget to pay your light bill. You need a haircut. You'll get one tomorrow. You would wash your clothes, but you aren't certain how much detergent to put in the washing machine and you don't have any change. You would like to have another dog. (Despite the fact that Plato had shown his allegiance to Paula in the end, a dog is a wonderful companion for a newly divorced man. A dog, unlike a woman, waits patiently and never asks where you have been when you come home late, and a dog loves you and wags his tail and licks your hand, no matter what sort of company you have been keeping.) But who would feed a dog in case you didn't come home one night? The commode clogs up. You go to the restroom at the service station down the street. Maybe the commode will unclog itself. You can't find an ashtray, so you dump cigarettes into half-empty beer cans. Later you think you are reaching for a fresh beer, but you get the one with the cigarettes in it. If you ever decide to quit smoking, you know how you will do it—by drinking beer that has cigarettes floating in it. Even if your commode did work, it wouldn't matter, because you never have any toilet paper. You never seem to get around to putting your albums back into their proper covers. You never seem to get all the drawers in your chest pushed in at the same time. The living room floor disappears under a cover of yellowing newsprint. You can never quite get rid of your bad cold, and you can never think to buy shampoo, so you wash your hair with soap and you get a bad case of dandruff. You are able to grow incredibly healthy cultures in the bottom of unwashed coffee cups, but your one house plant dies.

Your social life, what there is of it, goes about the same way. Somebody gives you a free ticket to a concert and you can't find a date. You get a live date and your car battery goes dead on the way to pick her up. A ravishing young woman comes to work in your office. She dates a wrestler.

A newly divorced man learns. Or relearns, a lot of things, too, when he reenters the single life. He learns to eat a lot of Chinese food, because it comes in boxes that do not have to be washed. He learns to scratch his own back by standing next to a door and rubbing his back up against it, as a hog will do to a fence post. He learns that things still go bump in the night when he sleeps alone. He learns to hug a pillow when he is sleeping alone and things are going bump in the night. He learns never to wash a red shirt with his white underwear, or he will have pink underwear. He learns wearing pink underwear can lead to all sorts of embarrassing situations. He learns Sunday nights are the worst nights of the week.

I've never been quite sure what it is about Sunday nights. Monday nights, maybe there's a ball game on television. Tuesday nights, I meet a friend after work. We hit a few bars and eat midnight breakfast at the Dunk 'n' Dine. Wednesday nights, I get lucky at a happy hour. Thursday nights, I recover from Wednesday nights. Friday nights are New Year's Eve. Saturday nights, they play the music loud. Sunday nights, the locusts come.

My dislike for Sunday nights began when I was a boy, that horrid summer my mother would leave me on Sunday nights to go back to school. And even after she stopped leaving, she never cooked on Sunday nights. It was the one night a week that I had to fend for myself, foraging through the refrigerator in search of some morsel, such as a cold chicken wing, left over from Sunday lunch. Television has always been lousy on Sunday nights, too. (See earlier reference to "The Ed Sullivan Show.") Sunday nights, the world keeps to itself. The bars close. The bus station is empty. The first six days of the week pass with an evergrowing flourish of promise. Sunday nights linger on and on and throw a black shroud over any manifestation of optimism. Nobody dances on Sunday nights.

Sunday nights, I didn't want my freedom anymore. I wanted to be a little boy again, nestled innocently against my mother's side. I wanted Paula back on Sunday nights. I wanted her in my bed, and I wanted her back turned toward me, so I could press myself against her, fitting almost perfectly with every contour of her body. I wanted to sleep with my mouth against the back of her neck, breathing in the smell of her hair. Six nights a week, I could be a gypsy and roam free. Sunday nights, I wanted a home.

*   *   *

I was one of them now, the single set, the unattached, the wanderers of Peachtree Street, who celebrated six nights of sundowns together. While the others lived in the timid security of the suburbs, settling for the even pace of marriage and commitment, we took to that oft-noted fast-lane. For those who have never tried it, let me explain the lure:

You can do it with numbers, i.e., put thrill and moments to remember on a scale of one to a hundred. A root canal job at the dentist's office, for example, would be one. Spending a passionate night with a beautiful woman, who would cook you breakfast the next morning and do your eggs exactly the way you like them would rank about a ninety-seven. If her daddy happened to own a liquor store, that might rank a perfect hundred.

Married life has its ups and downs, too, but usually things go along at a fairly even clip.

When I was married, I usually was doing about a fifty-five on the thrill-and-moment-to-remember scale.

But single. Certainly being single has its low points, but there always is that chance that you will walk into a crowded bar, step into an elevator, or sit down in an airplane and, subsequently, roar into the eighties or nineties. Here are some things that can happen to you when you are single, and the approximate position each experience would have on the scale:

—Waking up Monday morning to find the roads are iced over and you don't have to go to work: eighty-one.

—You're out of coffee: eleven.

—Your neighbor, who is gorgeous, is also stuck in her apartment: seventy-three.

—Her boyfriend owns a four-wheel-drive vehicle: eight.

—A woman you used to date, who moved away a year ago, calls and says she's in town for a few days and wants to get together with you: seventy-four.

—She's put on twenty-five pounds since you saw her last: nine.

—You sit down at a table in a bar with two gorgeous secretaries you've never seen before: sixty-one.

—They're from a small town and in the city for a convention: sixty-five.

—They haven't heard any of your jokes: sixty-eight.

—They both have large breasts: seventy-three.

—They're on expense account: seventy-seven.

—The one on your left constantly tries to make eye contact with you: eighty-three.

—The one on your right is rubbing her leg against yours under the table: eighty-seven.

—They're both getting very drunk: eighty-nine.

—They've already had dinner: ninety-one.

—Now the one on your left is rubbing your other leg with hers under the table: ninety-four.

—You don't have to go to the bathroom: ninety-five.

—They begin to kiss you on your ears simultaneously: ninety-eight.

—An old friend from college, who played two seasons with the Dodgers and now models men's undershorts, spots you and joins the table: fourteen.

There is also new terminology to learn once one has joined the night-fliers and fast-laners. Mostly, it has to do with the ongoing attempt never to be caught without suitable feminine companionship after midnight, for to do so is terribly damaging to the single male's fragile ego. Being alone late is at the very bottom of the number scale, a situation to be avoided at all costs. There are several lengths to which a single or divorced man will go to make certain this misfortune doesn't befall him, and there is a proper term for each exercise.

SAFETY VALVE: What the term implies. Never go out into a bar in search of companionship without having something in reserve. A safety valve is usually a woman from whom one has taken comfort before. There is nothing particularly wrong with a safety valve, it's just that time and familiarity have moved her into a position of backup, behind possible starters one might find in an evening's singles bar shopping. Normally, a safety is handled this way:

"Hi, it's me."

"What's up?"

"I was just checking to see if you're doing anything later on this evening."

"Not that I know of."

"Well, I've got this meeting to go to and I was wondering, if I got out in time, could I call you and maybe come over?"

"What time do you think you'll be out of your meeting?"

"I'm not sure."

"Well, as long as it's not too late. I've got to get up early in the morning."

"If it's too late, I won't call."

This is the ideal situation. If you happen to run into something new and exciting, the meeting ran until past eleven. If you don't, no problem. The safety valve is only a phone call away.

Having a safety allows a man to be more at ease in the early hours of the evening, when he is in the midst of his search, because there is little or no pressure. The more desperate the hunter, the less likely he is to find game. Or, never climb to the high wire without a net to catch you if you fall.

GOING TO THE WHIP: This is, in fact, a move of desperation. You have no safety valve. The only thing moving in the bars are Xerox salesmen in three-piece suits. All your friends have dates. You ask the bartender for a handful of change and you spend the rest of the evening in the phone booth, dialing and hoping.

BLACK CORD FEVER: The most desperate of all situations. It is one o'clock in the morning and you are lying in your bed, staring at the ceiling. You have perhaps had several cocktails during the evening, but otherwise it has been a total snake-eyes sort of night.

Before you can go to sleep, you must talk to someone, anyone, as long as she happens to be female. You look at the telephone. You realize it is the middle of the night, but it doesn't matter.

You dial. The phone rings on the other end. She answers.

"Hi there!" you chirp.

"Whatimeizit?" she asks.

"The night is yet young," you reply.

"Who is this?"

You tell her.

"What do you want?"

You say you are lonely and you just wanted to talk.

She says you are a rotten so-and-so, and you have no business waking her up at this ungodly hour.

You apologize, but say you have been thinking about her all evening and absolutely had to call.

Suddenly the man who was sleeping next to her is on the phone, and he informs you that if you ever call there again at *any* hour, he is going to take a phone and make it an integral part of your body.

He slams the phone down. You dial another number; that's Black Cord fever.

CLOSING THE DEAL: Meeting a girl in a bar and convincing her to leave with you.

FIRING A BLANK: Meeting a girl in a bar and *not* being able to convince her to leave with you.

TAP CITY: You don't get her phone number, either.

GEOGRAPHICALLY UNDESIRABLE: Also affectionately known as "G.U." This is a girl you meet in a bar on the north side of town, and she is divorced and got the house, which is located thirty miles away in some distant suburb, a sixty mile roundtripper. And when you get to her house, she might make you sleep on the couch. In Atlanta, "G.U.'s" generally live in Stone Mountain, Lilburn, Jonesboro, across the Chattahoochee River in Roswell, Powder Springs, and, God forbid, Villa Rica.

CARD SMOOTHERS: These are girls who haven't had dinner yet when you meet them, and they want to go to one of those places where they put a lot of sauce on the food, serve the green beans raw, and cook the tomatoes. These are usually young, blonde girls with nice tans, who drive convertibles, know the difference between French and domestic champagnes, and prefer the former. They will wear the writing right off your plastic credit card.

COYOTES: These are girls who didn't look all that bad when you went home with them in your drunken stupor the night before. The next morning when you awaken, however, you are horrified at what you are holding in your arms. The term "coyote" comes from the possibility that you can wake up with a woman so unsightly, you would gnaw your arm off rather than move it and risk awakening her.

THREES: Never attempt to make any sort of headway with a girl in a bar if she is accompanied by two friends. They all came in the same car. One will be ugly and constantly urging the other two to leave. The other will be a mother-hen type who doesn't want to see her friend taken advantage of. She will keep a watchful eye on you every moment, and will go off to the restroom with the object of your affection and tell her you look married. Twos can be a problem, too, but they are much less cumbersome than threes. With twos, there is the distinct possibility somebody will fire on her friend. If she happens to be ugly, though, forget it. Any attempt to talk the pretty one out of the place will be met with a whispered, "I just can't leave Betty Ann."

COUNTRY GIRLS: Forget it. All they want to do is *daintz*.

Do not get the idea, however, that the singles bar and dating-after-a-divorce scene is one-sided. Women play their own games. Here are some examples.

RAIN CHECKS: Most women will never tell you flatly that they think you are a total turkey and they have no interest in you whatsoever. Instead, they will leave you dangling with your ill-founded hopes by saying, "Oh, I'd love to go out with you Monday night, but I've already got plans. Can I take a rain check?

"Tuesday night? No, I've got exercise class that night. Could I take a rain check?"

"Wednesday night? No, I'm flying Wednesday through Friday. Could I take a. . . . etc."

CATS: Women don't really like cats. They just use the little boogers as excuses for not going out with you. If you ask a woman out and she says, "I'd love to, but I've got to take my cat to the vet," she's noticed you have bad breath. If she says, "I'd love to, but I have to give my cat a bath," it means she'd rather do anything under the sun than go out with you, even bathe a cat.

Women also use cats as birth control devices. If you go home with a woman and she has a cat in the house, the cat immediately will become angered at your intrusion and will jump on your head and back whenever you attempt to become even the slightest bit romantic. If the lights happen to be off and you are in bed at the time, a cat jumping on your head and back will frighten you right out of the mood for any further passion.

MENSTRUAL CRAMPS: Women will use menstrual cramps to explain away any sort of intemperate behavior, as in, "I'm sorry I was so bitchy last night and flushed your wallet down the toilet when we had that fight. It's just that these cramps. . . ." What is frightening about that, is women can reach a point where they figure they can get away with anything because they had menstrual cramps. "I know I took an ax and chopped up my date last night, your honor, but it's just that these cramps. . . ." If a woman tells you she is having menstrual cramps, go immediately to the nearest drugstore and buy a box of Midol tablets. Swallow four as quickly as you can.

POPCORN: Whenever you take a woman to a movie, she will never indicate a desire for her own box of popcorn.

"How about a box of popcorn?" you will ask her.

"No, thanks," she will inevitably reply. "I'll just eat some of yours."

It is impossible to convince a woman that you want an entire box of popcorn yourself, and have no qualms about spending enough money so she can have a box of her own, even if she eats only a handful of it.

I think this stems from the belief most women have that they can eat and not gain weight if they follow certain guidelines. Even the thinnest women are afraid of gaining one ounce of weight, which has enabled a great many talentless people to write a great many diet books. Women believe they will *not* gain weight if:

—They eat popcorn out of *your* box, or they eat French fries off *your* plate, or they spoon a glob of ice cream off *your* dish.

—They eat fattening foods while standing up.

—They eat fattening foods in the kitchen, rather than eating them at the table with everybody else.

—They eat in bed.

—They eat Oreo cookies in order to ease their menstrual cramps.

MOVING: When a man has to move to a new location, he either calls Mayflower or rents a truck and does the work himself. A woman goes to singles bars and recruits.

"Hi, I'm Shirley. Remember, we met at Harrison's the other night?"

"Sure, Shirley, I remember you."

"Well, I was just wondering if you had any plans Saturday afternoon?"

''Me? No, I don't have any plans at all. What do you have in mind?''

''Well, I'm moving to this great new apartment, and I was wondering if you would mind helping me move? I don't have very much, except for the piano. . . .''

BABYSITTING: Naturally, the girls I dated in high school and college never had any children. Out there in the adult world, however, there are a lot of unattached women with kids. Women with children have to be home at a certain hour, because they have babysitters. They often will allow you to follow them home from a bar—after you have paid the check, of course—and then ask you for babysitter money. After you have paid the babysitter, you can sit on the couch and neck for a few moments, amidst the toys and puzzles the kids left out. But that's about all you will get, because there are children in the house, and to go any farther risks the kids telling their daddy that mommy has been fooling around. On the way out to your car, you slip on a Big Wheel and twist your ankle.

If you date a woman who has children, you will attempt to make friends with the kids, thinking this will impress their mother. She couldn't care less. However, if you do show an interest in the children, whether genuine or not, she will then take advantage of you by occasionally asking you to babysit with them while she goes out to run a few errands. This happened to an acquaintance of mine, who discovered he was being used as a babysitter in the vilest sort of way. He explained:

''This all began when I bought her some new boots,'' he began. ''We were window shopping and she saw this pair of boots she liked. The next day, I went back to the store, bought them for her, and surprised her with them.

"A week or so later, she called me one afternoon and asked me to go over and be at her apartment when the kids came home from school. She said she had to work a little late and would be home as soon as she got off from work.

"Like the fool I was, I went over to the house and was there when the kids got home. The little boy kicked me in the shins, and the little girl spit on me when I tried to get her to turn down the TV.

"I was there an hour and then two hours, and then I called their mother's office. No answer. I became suspicious. I put the two little devils in the back of my car and I started driving around to neighborhood bars, looking for their mother. I would run in one and then run back out, so the children wouldn't have time to destroy my car while I was gone.

"The fourth spot I went into was very dark. I couldn't see anybody's face, but suddenly, I noticed a couple sitting over in a corner making out. The woman's form looked very familiar, but I couldn't tell for sure. Then I looked at her feet. I saw my boots. I didn't say anything, but I got even. I took the kids back home and let them try to make fudge. I doubt if she ever got the chocolate off the kitchen wallpaper."

*   *   *

I had a lot of experiences after I divorced. Some were even wonderful. I met a French Canadian girl in Montreal and went for carriage rides with her. I was in Maxwell's Plum in New York one night and charmed a young woman with my Southern accent, and she took me to her house in Tarrytown. I met a girl on an all-night train ride who didn't have a sleeper. I did. I met girls who cooked me wonderful meals. I met girls who rubbed my back. I met girls with pretty smiles who laughed at all my stories, and didn't tell me when I forgot and repeated them. And then I met Kay.

XIV

'...forsaking all
others...'

S HE HAD THOSE eyes, those big, sparkling eyes. She snorted through her nose when she laughed. She sang to me. I would sit on the floor with her, and she would play her guitar and she would sing for me in a South Carolina, low-country accent that could have made any angel's chorus.

She sang "Clouds," and "Leaving on a Jet Plane," and "Nobody Knows You When You're Down and Out." She had an innocence about her. She was young and fresh and new in the city. I took her out that first time. We went to Underground Atlanta and we danced. We danced over and over again, and the last dance was something slow, and we held each other very close. I kissed her on her neck, and then we just stopped in the middle of the dance floor, and I kissed her on the mouth, and I didn't care who saw us—let them eat their hearts out that they are not as lucky as we.

We had some times, we did. She wore funny hats that she pulled down over her ears. She looked like a little girl when she did that. I used to have this thing about fuzzy puppies. I would hold a fuzzy puppy and I would have an urge to clutch it to me as closely as I could, and I would want to squeeze it and give it every ounce of my affection. I wanted to do that to Kay. I wanted to smother her with my arms. Those eyes. God, those eyes.

I weighed it all. I had been married once and it hadn't worked out. I'd been restless and eager to run. There had been all that agony of the parting, all that heartbreak and all those regrets.

But I was too young then. I hadn't had my time to run unbridled. But that was behind me now. I had answered the call of the wild neon. I had done my dances and told my stories for three years since my divorce. What was left out there for me to gain? Just more of the same. Night after night, searching and never quite finding. Hard mornings. Aching heads and growling stomachs. Loud music and quiet moments to wonder if I would still remember what to do if it ever stopped playing. I was sick and tired of waking up sick and tired.

As much as I had tried, I had never gotten over my fear of being caught, to digress, late and alone. Those nights in my grandparents' house I cried myself to sleep missing my mother. Those nights on the sofa when my new stepfather took my place in the bed beside her. The night that Paula left and the room closed in on me. The night I found her note that she was leaving again. A hundred other such nights, a thousand other such nights from my past. They hung over me, daring me to test myself against them again.

There is nothing harsher than a lonely night alone. There is no warmth. No peace. Demons dance and fearful shadows cavort. Little boys who are afraid of the dark grow up to be men who dread the end of late, late shows. They wrestle the night and rarely give in to it.

I had paid a big price for my freedom. I wanted to flourish in it. I wanted to be my own, spirited man, needing not the protective wing of a woman. But it was clear to me, ever and ever more clear to me, that I did not possess such strength, and I doubt very few men ever do. The comfort of the alternative is too great to be without it very long.

*   *   *

Kay wore a blue dress, and her hand was trembling when I took it in mine. It was what she wanted, she said. And it was what I thought I wanted, too.

It would be different this time. The dilemma of my past was behind me. I, Lewis, would take this woman for my wife, forsaking all others until death did us part, and hang me in the public square and let the birds peck out my eyes if I ever so much as had one fleeting thought of doing otherwise.

We took the train to Ft. Lauderdale for our honeymoon. We called our parents the next morning to tell them what we had done. My mother asked me, "Are you sure?"

I said, "I'm sure."

I suppose she believed me.

Kay's father wired flowers and sent champagne.

We stretched out in the sun and we ran into the surf, and I threw her into the waves. She sang songs to me. I made up silly poems for her.

We came home a week later. I drove past Harrison's one afternoon, and I saw a friend's car parked outside. We had two, maybe three, and then he said let's have one more.

I put the dime in the slot a couple of hours later. When Kay answered, I said I would be home in a couple of minutes.

Epilogue

Epilogue

PAULA IS STILL married to her second husband. She also had another baby.

Kay and I divorced in 1976.

I divorced for the third time in 1982; I'm not exactly sure why. But we did get into a huge fight one morning while waiting for a train in Paris.

Mama Willie, Uncle John Wesley, Hugh Dorsey, and Plato all died.

My mother and my stepfather still live in Moreland. My mother wishes she had some grandchildren.

I hired a maid and bought a microwave oven.

Harrison's opened a second bar in Atlanta. It's packed most nights.

Also by Robert M. Sapolsky

The Trouble with Testosterone
and Other Essays on the Biology of the Human Predicament

Why Zebras Don't Get Ulcers:
A Guide to Stress, Stress-Related Diseases, and Coping

Stress, the Aging Brain, and the Mechanisms of Neuron Death

A Primate's Memoir

Robert M. Sapolsky

A TOUCHSTONE BOOK
PUBLISHED BY SIMON & SCHUSTER
New York   London   Toronto   Sydney

To Benjamin and Rachel

TOUCHSTONE
Rockefeller Center
1230 Avenue of the Americas
New York, NY 10020

First Touchstone Edition 2002
TOUCHSTONE and colophon are registered trademarks of Simon & Schuster, Inc.
For information about special discounts for bulk purchases,
please contact Simon & Schuster Special Sales:
1-800-456-6798 or business@simonandschuster.com
DESIGN BY ERICH HOBBING
Set in Adobe Garamond
Manufactured in the United States of America

17 19 20 18

The Library of Congress has cataloged the Scribner edition as follows:
Sapolsky, Robert M.
A primate's memoir/Robert M. Sapolsky.
p. cm.
1. Baboons—Behavior—Africa, East—Anecdotes.
2. Sapolsky, Robert M.
I. Title.

QL737.P93 S27 2001
599.8'6515'09676—dc21.
00-063522

ISBN-13: 978-0-7432-0247-3
ISBN-10:   0-7432-0247-3
ISBN-13: 978-0-7432-0241-1 (Pbk)
ISBN-10:   0-7432-0241-4 (Pbk)

The names and other identifying characteristics of some people have been changed.

CONTENTS

Part 3: Tenuous Adulthood

Part 4: Adulthood

ACKNOWLEDGMENTS

This is a memoir of my more than twenty years spent working intermittently in a national park in East Africa. The stories are true but, as is often the case in such retellings, subject to a bit of literary license that I want to describe here. The story of Wilson Kipkoi is true in most details. However, names and some other details have been changed to protect anonymity. The final chapter, unfortunately, is true in all its devastating details; however, here, too, I have changed names and certain characteristics. The chronology of the various chapters has been expanded in some places, truncated in others. In a few cases, the sequence of some stories has been changed; the sequence of all events in the lives of the baboons, however, is unchanged. Finally, a number of humans, and a number of baboons, represent composites of a few members of their species. This was done to keep down the cast of characters coming and going—for example, within the human realm, a particular game-park ranger, British tour operator, or tourist-lodge waiter may be a composite of a few individuals. All of the major baboon figures are real individuals, as are the major human characters—Richard, Hudson, Laurence of the Hyenas, (the late) Rhoda, Samwelly, Soirowa, Jim Else, Mbarak Suleman, Ross Tarara, and, of course, Lisa are all real people. I, to the best of my knowledge, am not a composite.

A number of individuals helped me with fact checking, reading part or all of this book or, in the case of Soirowa, who cannot read, having sections in it related, in order to confirm the accuracy of facts as they remember them. As such, I thank Jim Else, Laurence Frank, Richard Kones, Hudson Oyaro, and Soirowa. I also thank Colin Warner for some formal fact checking in the library, and John McLaughlin, Anne Meyer, Miranda Ip, and Mani Roy for help in proofreading the manuscript. Thanks also to Robert Shanafelt for pointing out an error in the finished volume. Dan Greenwood and Carol Salem shared stories with me of their travels in East Africa, and I thank them for that. I thank Jonathan Cobb, Liz Ziemska, and Patricia Gadsby for their priceless editorial advice when reading what was a proto-version of this book, a number of years ago.

Funding for this work was made possible by the Explorer's Club, the Harry Frank Guggenheim Foundation, the MacArthur Foundation, and the Templeton Foundation. I thank them not only for their generosity but for their extraordinary flexibility in recognizing the peculiar exigencies of fieldwork— at the very least, I thank them for accepting receipts and budget summaries on waterlogged, moth-eaten (literally) accounting notebooks. I thank the Institute of Primate Research, National Museums of Kenya, for my association with them, and the Office of the President, Republic of Kenya, for permission to conduct my research all these years. Two colleagues—Shirley Strum of the University of California at San Diego, and Jeanne Altmann, of Princeton University, have opened their field sites to me as part of our collaborations, and I thank them for that experience. And I thank a number of individuals who taught me aspects of doing fieldwork or helped me with data collection during some of the early seasons—Davie Brooks, Denise Costich, Francis Onchiri, and Reed Sutherland.

I thank my agent, Katinka Matson, for her tremendous support and expertise in making this book a reality, and Gillian Blake, my editor, and Rachel Sussman, her assistant—you have been remarkably graceful in pointing out problems in this manuscript that anyone but a scientist should have learned back in Creative Writing 101. It has been a pleasure working with you all.

And finally, I thank my wife, Lisa, the love of my life, who has shared so many of these moments in Kenya with me.

A final note: The depredations and plunderings of colonialism in Africa are now a thing of the past. However, the West often continues to exploit Africa in far subtler ways, even on those occasions when intentions are the best. I have now spent more than half my life connected with Africa, and I have intense feelings of warmth, respect, and gratitude for the place and my friends there. I deeply hope that I have not inadvertently been exploitative in any way in these writings. This was the last thing I would have intended.

Part 1

The Adolescent Years:

When I First Joined the Troop

1

The Baboons:
The Generations of Israel

I joined the baboon troop during my twenty-first year. I had never planned to become a savanna baboon when I grew up; instead, I had always assumed I would become a mountain gorilla. As a child in New York, I endlessly begged and cajoled my mother into taking me to the Museum of Natural History, where I would spend hours looking at the African dioramas, wishing to live in one. Racing effortlessly across the grasslands as a zebra certainly had its appeal, and on some occasions, I could conceive of overcoming my childhood endomorphism and would aspire to giraffehood. During one period, I became enthused with the collectivist utopian rants of my elderly communist relatives and decided that I would someday grow up to be a social insect. A worker ant, of course. I made the miscalculation of putting this scheme into an elementary-school writing assignment about my plan for life, resulting in a worried note from the teacher to my mother.

Yet, whenever I wandered the Africa halls in the museum, I would invariably return to the mountain gorilla diorama. Something primal had clicked the first time I stood in front of it. My grandfathers had died long before I was born. They were mythically distant enough that I would not be able to pick either out in a picture. Amid this grandfatherly vacuum, I decided that a real-life version of the massive, sheltering silverback male gorilla stuffed in the glass case would be a good substitute. A mountainous African rain forest amid a group of gorillas began to seem like the greatest refuge imaginable.

By age twelve, I was writing fan letters to primatologists. By fourteen, I was reading textbooks on the subject. Throughout high school, I finagled jobs in a primate lab at a medical school and, finally, sojourning to Mecca itself, volunteered in the primate wing of the museum. I even forced the chairman of my high school language department to find me a self-paced course in Swahili, in preparation for the fieldwork I planned to do in Africa. Eventually, I went off to college to study with one of the deans of primatology. Everything seemed to be falling into place.

But in college, some of my research interests shifted and I became focused on scientific questions that could not be answered with gorillas. I would need to study a species that lived out in the open in the grasslands, with a different type of social organization, a species that was not endangered. Savanna baboons, who had struck no particular chord in me before, became the logical species to study. You make compromises in life; not every kid can grow up to become president or a baseball star or a mountain gorilla. So I made plans to join the baboon troop.

I joined the troop in the last year of the reign of Solomon. In those days, the other central members of the troop were Leah, Devorah, Aaron, Isaac, Naomi, and Rachel. I didn't plan beforehand to give the baboons Old Testament names. It just happened. A new adult male, leaving the troop he grew up in, would transfer into the troop, and during the few weeks when he'd vacillate about joining permanently, I would hesitate about giving him a name. I'd just refer to him in my notes as the new adult transfer, or NAT, or Nat, or, by the time he decided to stay forever, Nathanial. Adam was first known as ATM, for adult transfer male. The small kid who was first abbreviated as the SML kid then turned into Samuel on me. At that point I just gave up and started handing out the prophets and matriarchs and judges left and right. I would still occasionally stick with a purely descriptive name—Gums or Limp, for example. And I was way too insecure in my science to publish technical papers using these names—everyone got a number then. But the rest of the time, I wallowed in biblical names.

I have always liked Old Testament names, but I would hesitate to inflict Obadiah or Ezekial on a child of mine, so I ran wild with the sixty baboons in the troop. Plus, clearly, I was still irritated by the years I spent toting my Time-Life books on evolution to show my Hebrew school teachers, having them blanch at such sacrilege and tell me to put them away; it felt like a pleasing revenge to hand out the names of the patriarchs to a bunch of baboons on the African plains. And, with some sort of perversity that I suspect powers a lot of what primatologists do, I couldn't wait for the inevitable day that I could record in my field notebook that Nebuchanezzar and Naomi were off screwing in the bushes.

What I wanted to study was stress-related disease and its relationship to behavior. Sixty years ago, a scientist named Selye discovered that your emotional life can affect your health. It struck the mainstream doctors as ludicrous—people were perfectly accustomed to the idea of viruses or bacteria or carcinogens or whatnot getting you sick, but your emotions? Selye found that if you got rats upset in all sorts of purely psychological ways, they got sick. They got ulcers, their immune systems collapsed, their reproduction went to hell, they got high blood pressure. We know now exactly what was happening—this was the discovery of stress-related disease. Selye showed that stress was what you were undergoing when emotional or physical disturbances threw your body's balance out of whack. And if it went on for too long, you got sick.

That last piece has been hammered home with a vengeance—stress makes all sorts of things in the body go bad, and in the years since Selye, people have documented numerous diseases that can be worsened by stress. Adult onset diabetes, muscle atrophy, high blood pressure and atherosclerosis, arrested growth, impotency, amenorrhea, depression, decalcification of bones. You name it. In my laboratory work, I was studying how, on top of all that, stress can kill certain brain cells.

It seemed a miracle that any of us survived. But clearly we did. I decided that, in addition to my laboratory work on neurons, I wanted to study the optimistic side of it—how come some of us are more resistant to stress than others? Why are some bodies and some psyches better at coping? Does it have something to do with your rank in society? If you have lots of relatives, if you hang out with friends? If you play with kids? If you sulk when you're upset about something or if you find someone else to take it out on? I decided to go study this in wild baboons.

They were perfect for it. Baboons live in big, complex social groups, and the population I went to study lived like kings. Great ecosystem, the Serengeti. Grass and trees and animals forever, Marlin Perkins country. The baboons work maybe four hours a day to feed themselves; hardly anyone is likely to eat them. Basically, baboons have about a half dozen solid hours of sunlight a day to devote to being rotten to each other. Just like our society—few of us are getting hypertensive from physical stressors, none of us are worrying about famines or locust plagues or the ax fight we're going to have with the boss out in the parking lot at five o'clock. We live well enough to have the luxury to get ourselves sick with purely social, psychological stress. Just like these baboons.

So I would go out and study the behavior of baboons, see who was doing what with whom—fights, trysts and friendships, alliances and dalliances. Then I would dart them, anesthetize them, see how their bodies were doing—blood pressure, cholesterol levels, rate of wound healing, levels of stress hormones. What would individual differences in behavior and psychological patterns have to do with the individual differences in how their bodies were working? I wound up studying only the males. You wouldn't want to anesthetize females when they were pregnant, or when they had a dependent nursing kid, and that's most of the time for most of the females. Thus, I settled in with the males and planned to get to know them very well.

It was 1978; John Travolta was the most important human alive, white suits were sweeping our proud nation, and Solomon was in the final year of his rule. Solomon was good and wise and just. Actually, that's nonsense, but I was an impressionable young transfer male at the time. Nevertheless, he was a pretty imposing baboon. For years, the anthropology textbooks had been having a love affair with savanna baboons and their top-ranking male, the alpha male. According to the books, the baboons were complex social primates living in open grasslands; they had organized hunts, a hierarchical rank system, and at their core was the alpha male. He led the troop to food, spearheaded the hunts, defended against predators, kept the females in line, changed the lightbulbs, fixed the car, blah blah blah. Just like our human ancestors, the textbooks ached to say, and sometimes even did. Most of that turned out to be wrong, naturally. The hunts for food were disorganized free-for-alls. Furthermore, the alpha male couldn't lead the troop to food during a crisis, as he wouldn't know where to go. The males transferred into the troops as adolescents, while the females spent their whole lives in the same troop. Thus, it would be the old females who remembered the grove of olive trees past the fourth hill. When predators attacked, the alpha male would be in the thick of it, defending an infant. But only if he was absolutely certain that it was his kid who was at risk of becoming someone's dinner. Otherwise, he had the highest, safest spot in the tree to watch the action. So much for Robert Ardrey and 1960s anthropology.

Nevertheless, within the small, parochial, self-interested, unreflective, petty world of male baboons, being alpha was hot stuff. You might not really be the troop leader, but you got to do about half the matings, sit in the shade when it was hot, enjoy the best food with a minimum of effort merely by ripping off someone else's lunch box. And Solomon excelled at all of this. He had been alpha male in the troop for three years, an inordinately long time for a male's tenure. The grad student who preceded me with the troop said that Solomon had been a ferocious and canny fighter back when he defeated his predecessor, but by the time I got there (and secretly instituted the name Solomon—his boring published identification number I will never divulge), he was in his silver years and resting on his laurels, persisting out of sheer psychological intimidation. He was damn good at it. He hadn't had a major fight in a year. He would just glance at someone, rouse himself from his regal setting and saunter over, at the most swat him, and that would settle things. Everyone was terrified of him. He swatted at me once, knocked me off a rock, shattered my going-away-to-Africa-gift binoculars, left me terrified of him as well. I immediately dropped any plans I might have had of challenging him for the alpha position.

Most of his days he spent lounging with the many infants who he felt certain were his kids (i.e., no one else went near the female baboon during the part of the cycle she conceived), stealing the occasional tuber or root that someone else had dug up, being groomed, consorting with new females in heat. As of late, the hot number in the troop was Devorah, daughter of Leah, who was probably the oldest member of the troop, the alpha female, and one incredibly tough cookie. Male baboon ranks shift over time; as someone grows into his prime, someone else snaps a canine and is out of business. Females, on the other hand, inherit their rank from their mothers; they get the rank below mom, kid sister gets one below that, and so on, until the next lower-ranking family starts. So Leah had been sitting on top of that pile for at least a quarter of a century. Leah would harass Naomi, around her age and the matriarch of a much lower-ranking family. Old Naomi would sit down to a midday rest in some nice spot in the shade, and Leah would bash on over and boot her out. Naomi, unruffled, would find someplace else to sit, and, unable to resist, Leah would do it again and again. I would marvel at the antiquity of it. Some years before, Jimmy Carter was jogging at the White House, people were buying Pet Rocks and trying to look like Farrah Fawcett-Majors, and the aging Leah was giving Naomi grief. Even further back, the My Lai massacre occurred, people were wearing cranberry bell-bottoms and dancing on waterbeds, and the prime-aged Leah was forcing Naomi to groom her. Further back, Lyndon Johnson was showing off his gallbladder scar while the adolescent Leah was waiting for Naomi to fall asleep during her midday nap before hassling her. And way back when people were still protesting the Rosenbergs' being executed and I was positioned in my grandmother's lap in her nursing home for us to be photographed with the Brownie camera, Naomi, the toddler, had to give the branch she was playing with to Leah. And now they were two decrepit old ladies still playing musical chairs in the savanna.

Leah had given birth to a whole line of strapping, confident sons. In various social species of animals, either males or females pick up and move to a different social group around puberty—one of those incest avoidance deals. Among baboons, it's the males who get this undefined itch of wanderlust, and Leah's sons were raising havoc far and wide throughout the troops of the northeast

Serengeti. Devorah was her first daughter in quite some time, maybe even ever. She was just hitting puberty, and Solomon was going wild about her. Devorah was highly desirable by any male baboon's standards. She was well fed, in good health, and thus very likely to conceive and carry through her pregnancy. And once the kid was born, no one was going to mess with it; it would survive. From the standpoint of evolutionary theory, of leaving as many copies of your genes in future generations as possible, all that jazz, this was one highly desirable young primate. I never thought that Devorah was a big deal (unlike Bathsheeba, whom I had a crush on, and who was soon to meet a tragic end at the canines of that bastard Nebuchanezzar), but she certainly did not lack for confidence. When male baboons who are getting along well run into each other and want to say howdy, they yank on each other's penises. I think it is, in effect, their way of saying, "We're getting along so well, I trust you so much for this one second, that I'm gonna let you yank on me." Like dogs rolling on their backs to let each other sniff at their crotches. Among male primates, this means trust. All the guys did it to the other guys that they were pals with. And in addition, Leah and Devorah would do penis-grab greetings on males. Only females I ever saw do it. I saw Devorah pull this off on Nebuchanezzar, around the time he first joined the troop. He comes sauntering along, having just spent the morning causing trouble and feeling pretty good about himself, passes this little ol' lady and her young daughter, Leah and Devorah, coming the other way, don't reckon he knows them yet, but he does the male baboon equivalent of tipping his hat—flashing his eyebrows—and this young thing reaches over, and, well, she just yanks his balls, good solid heft, and goes walking on with the old biddy. Nebuchanezzar actually crouched to get a better view of her departing rear end, perhaps to be certain that she wasn't really some fella who just came past.

Thus, Devorah was sailing through puberty without a care, without a hint of acned insecurities, Solomon just waiting for her to smell a little sexier, get a slightly larger estrus swelling, perhaps, before starting to squire her around. Such was not the destiny, however, of poor Ruth, also going through puberty at that time. Hers was the more usual adolescence. She was from an obscure, low-ranking lineage and had the constant, swiveling, nervous movements of someone who gets dumped on a lot. Years later, in middle age, she would still have an anxious hyperadrenal look, and her umpteen kids would have the same frazzled edge to them. But this year, her major problem was that she was slowly being driven mad by estrogen. Puberty had hit, and she was getting estrus swellings and steroids were poisoning her brain, and all she could think of was male baboons—but no one was interested in her. For about the first six